Women, sexuality and social control

Edited by

CAROL SMART
Department of Social Studies
Trent Polytechnic, Nottingham

and

BARRY SMART
Department of Sociological Studies
University of Sheffield

ROUTLEDGE & KEGAN PAUL
London, Boston and Henley

First published in 1978
by Routledge & Kegan Paul Ltd
39 Store Street,
London WC1E 7DD,
Broadway House,
Newtown Road,
Henley-on-Thames,
Oxon RG9 1EN and
9 Park Street,
Boston, Mass. 02108, USA
Reprinted in 1978 and 1979
Printed in Great Britain by
Lowe and Brydone Printers Ltd
Thetford, Norfolk

British Library Cataloguing in Publication Data

Women, sexuality and social control.
    1. Women - social conditions 2. Social control
    I. Smart, Carol II. Smart, Barry
    301.41'2   HQ1154   77-30401

ISBN 0 7100 8723 3

Contents

CONTRIBUTORS   vi

WOMEN AND SOCIAL CONTROL: An introduction   1
Carol Smart and Barry Smart

1 THE COERCION OF PRIVACY: A feminist perspective   8
   Tove Stang Dahl and Annika Snare

2 THE MYTH OF MALE PROTECTIVENESS AND THE LEGAL
   SUBORDINATION OF WOMEN: An historical analysis   27
   Albie Sachs

3 DOCTORS AND THEIR PATIENTS: The social control of
   women in general practice   41
   Michèle Barrett and Helen Roberts

4 WHO NEEDS PROSTITUTES? The ideology of male sexual needs   53
   Mary McIntosh

5 SEXUAL CODES AND CONDUCT: A study of teenage girls   65
   Deirdre Wilson

6 SEXIST ASSUMPTIONS AND FEMALE DELINQUENCY: An empirical
   investigation   74
   Lesley Shacklady Smith

7 ACCOUNTING FOR RAPE: Reality and myth in press reporting   87
   Carol Smart and Barry Smart

8 STUDYING RAPE: Integrating research and social change   104
   Julia R. Schwendinger and Herman Schwendinger

BIBLIOGRAPHY   112

INDEX   119

Contributors

MICHÈLE BARRETT

Department of Social Science and Humanities, The City University, London.

TOVE STANG DAHL

Institute of Criminology and Criminal Law, University of Oslo, Norway

MARY MCINTOSH

Department of Sociology, University of Essex

HELEN ROBERTS

School of Studies in Social Science University of Bradford

ALBIE SACHS

Faculty of Law University of Southampton

HERMAN SCHWENDINGER

Department of Sociology University of Nevada, Las Vegas

JULIA R. SCHWENDINGER

Department of Sociology University of Nevada, Las Vegas

BARRY SMART

Department of Sociological Studies University of Sheffield

CAROL SMART

Department of Social Studies Trent Polytechnic, Nottingham

LESLEY SHACKLADY SMITH

Department of Science and Humanities Braintree College of Further Education, Essex

ANNIKA SNARE

Institute of Criminology and Criminal Law University of Oslo, Norway

DEIRDRE WILSON

Department of Sociological and Political Studies, University of Salford

Women and social control

An introduction

Carol Smart and Barry Smart

The status, oppression and exploitation of women began to reappear as a controversial issue during the mid 1960s. Since then the Women's Movement has grown in strength, diversified, and provoked specific reforms in social policy and legislation as well as stimulated research and investigation into the forms of exploitation and inequality that women's oppression assumes. A token recognition of the extent to which women occupy a universally inferior position in society was reflected in the decision to make 1975 International Women's Year.(1) In the same year in Great Britain (excluding Northern Ireland) two important legislative reforms were enacted; the first was the Equal Pay Act (1970) which finally came into force on 29 December 1975, and the second was the Sex Discrimination Act. The extent to which these legislative changes have been, or indeed can be, fully effective in improving the employment position, income and general social status of women is controversial (see Coussins, 1976), but such legislation alone can, in any case, only effect changes in particular aspects of women's lives. For example, it is ineffective, indeed irrelevant, as far as private and ideological forms of oppression or exploitation are concerned. Moreover, not only is the recent legislation ineffective as far as the domestic sphere or private lives of women in the home are concerned, but in addition it deliberately defines as outside its terms of reference such important public issues as the discriminatory practices of the Department of Health and Social Security, for example the 'co-habitation rule' and unequal social security benefits (Coote and Gill, 1974), and the double standard of morality implicit in the criminal and legal processes, for example the laws regarding prostitution and rape (Smart, 1976).

The limited effectiveness of recent legislation serves to reveal the extent to which the primary sources of women's oppression are outside, or even beyond, judicial influence, that is to say rest within, or arise from, prevailing material conditions, cultural values, customs and social practices, such as the differential socialisation of male and female children within the family, schooling, forms of speech and language, media propagated stereotypes and numerous other seemingly innocuous social processes. We do not deny the relative importance of legislation, but wish to distance ourselves from those who perceive the solution to women's oppression to lie in piecemeal legislative reforms rather than in fundamental social and economic change. However, before one can begin to talk about transcending or eliminating the forms of oppression and social control to which women are subject, an understanding of the several dimensions of the social division between men and women is necessary. It is to particular aspects of the latter, to analyses of specific forms of social control to which women are subject, that the papers in this volume are directed.

The social control of women assumes many forms, it may be internal or external, implicit or explicit, private or public, ideological or repressive. Now although it *may* no longer be appropriate to talk of 'the problem that has no name'(2) when referring to the discontents of women, the Women's Movement having provided a voice and a language with which women may articulate their manifest grievances, there remains the problem of showing the existence of specific *covert* forms of oppression and control, and of revealing that their location lies in the public sphere rather than in the individual psychologies or personal lives of oppressed women. The forms of social control to which women are subject vary from primary socialisation within the family, and secondary socialisation (by peer groups, the education system, the media, etc.), which reinforces the ways of acting, thinking and feeling 'characteristic' of the female role, femininity and womanhood, to the more formal processes of institutional intervention through legislation by the State, the implementation of the law, the penal system and the criminal process. It is within the public and 'visible' areas of social control that women have been most active in fighting for greater equality. Undoubtedly, however, the more difficult forms of social control to address, especially with the eclipse of more manifest forms of sexual discrimination, are those that arise implicitly through socialisation. As one feminist writer has noted:

> the socialisation of boys and girls into contrasting personalities and roles has now a more significant part to play in the perpetuation of the social structure. In a society in which obvious discrimination is condemned, 'natural' sex differences help to preserve the separation of roles and thus the inequalities upon which the economic system still depends. (Sharpe, 1976, p.62)

'Natural' sex differences represent a source of legitimation of the separation of roles and social divisions between men and women in two ways, first, directly, in as much as there exist, in the present, clear physical differences and differing capacities only some of which are a consequence of different sexual characteristics, the remainder being the emergent product of historical processes of differential socialisation and opportunity. The second way in which the concept of 'natural' sex-difference appears is in the form of an ideology which overlays and helps perpetuate material differences between men and women. The direct appeal to nature as the source of gender differences serves to occlude the significance of successive historical epochs within which women's position has been changing, to render negligible the specific cultural determination of women's sexuality in the present and to diminish in importance the capitalist mode of production's requirement for women's private, domestic labour, the source of the reproduction of labour power.

The nature of the relationship between women's work in the home and capitalism only became a significant issue with the development of feminist analyses of women's isolation in the home and their concomitant separation from the world of remunerative work (cf. Zaretsky, 1976; Dalla Costa and James, 1973; Gardiner, 1975, 1976; Secombe, 1973). Only with the advent of the discussion of domestic labour theory and the status of housework has recognition been given to the importance of women's work within the home in reproducing labour power. That such work may not realise surplus value, that it may not therefore be truly productive labour has been a source of controversy, but that the capitalist mode of production is dependent upon women within the institution of the family (indeed requires that women remain within the family) performing two vital functions, namely the production and maintenance of the present and future labour force, as well as being principally responsible for the consumption of the goods produced, is incontrovertible. It can be seen therefore that the social control of women assumes both material and ideological forms and occurs in both public and private domains.

Clearly in a class-divided society both women and men are subject to material, repressive and ideological forms of social control, although they are usually affected differently, women being subjected to control principally within the private domain where they are in fact economically and legally subordinate to men. In addition, however, there are dimensions of social control which women alone experience; these are in relation to the following:

(a) the reproductive cycle;
(b) a double standard of morality;
(c) a subordinate social and legal status (vis-à-vis men) in the family;
(d) the separation of 'home' and 'work' and the ideology of woman's place.

THE REPRODUCTIVE CYCLE

In a highly individualistic society the state of being pregnant is generally conceived as a unique and individual event, in fact it has come to symbolise the 'fulfilment' of womanhood. The *reality* of pregnancy, however, is far removed from this ideal as the work of Graham (1976a and b), Macintyre (1976) and Oakley (1976) reveals. It is not that pregnancy often involves unpleasant physical and psychological side effects that primarily concerns us here, but rather the extent to which women are generally misinformed or ill-informed about the processes that follow from conception to birth, and the extent to which the manipulation of childbirth has become the domain of a male-dominated medical profession.

On the first point, Graham (1976a) has shown that women are subjected to ambiguous and contradictory images of pregnancy in handbooks on 'Mothercare'. In particular, she argues that the use of specific photographic techniques tends to romanticise pregnancy, constructs or produces an image in which the pregnant woman is *at one* with Nature, serene, content and somehow pure and non-sexual. Pregnant women are represented as constituting an homogeneous group, the imagery employed portrays them as of one race or ethnic group, one class or age and marital status, and as being in an economically unproblematic and carefree social environment. This conception of pregnancy contrasts sharply with the reality of medical practices such as internal examinations, attendance at impersonal, busy clinics and treatment in cold, sterile surroundings, circumstances which many pregnant women find alien, traumatic and distressing. Moreover, Graham (1976b) has shown the extent to which the experience of being pregnant, a potentiality or an actuality shared by almost *all* women, is highly privatised. Few women in her study felt they could (or should) discuss or share what were, in fact, commonly felt problems and worries, with the result that many pregnant women believed their anxieties were personal troubles rather than public issues. As Graham states, 'these problems, although shared, are not necessarily communicated - either to other pregnant women, to the family, to the doctor - for neither community nor clinic appear to recognise the existence or the salience of such concerns' (1976b, p.22).

In spite of major scientific advances in the fields of obstetrics and gynaecology, pregnancy is still subject to mystification. Yet perhaps it is more accurate to say that it is because of these major scientific advances that women are kept in ignorance of their own reproductive cycle. For as Oakley (1976) has argued the appropria- tion of the process of childbirth by the medical profession has had two important consequences. First, it has placed a completely female function in the hands of a profession which is heavily domin- ated by male ideology and which is not concerned with the emotional experience of giving birth, but more interested in efficient birth processes and the deployment of advanced technology. Consequently, the experience of giving birth in a hospital becomes a process over which pregnant women have little control, the organisation of repro- duction and the techniques and methods employed being determined by the medical profession in line with criteria which place the needs and interests of the hospital administration foremost. Second, the medical profession has tended to appropriate and monopolise medical knowledge of pregnancy and childbirth methods, and through a variety of restrictive practices to ensure that a hierarchical distribution of 'competence' and knowledge necessary for assisting in childbirth is maintained. The medical profession appears to expect pregnant women to defer unquestioningly to the authority of doctors, and to acquiesce or cede to the organisational requirements of hospital care. Consequently, women's knowledge of, and control over, their own bodies has diminished, whilst concomitantly the stock of medical knowledge has increased and the control of the medical profession has been extended.(3)

A DOUBLE STANDARD OF MORALITY

The concept of a double standard of morality refers to our code of sexual mores which persistently encourages or condones sexual prom- iscuity in men (and boys) as a display of 'masculinity' and male aggression, whilst condemning it in women (and girls) as a sign of 'unfeminine', shameful or pathological behaviour. Social control over human sexuality operates at several different levels, from the informal group processes to the institutional court procedures of our system of adult and juvenile justice. At the former level, the prime example of the differential control exercised over women is revealed in the language or words used to refer to the sexually promiscuous (see Adams and Laurikietis, 1976; Lakoff, 1975). The 'promiscuous' or simply the potentially 'promiscuous' woman or girl becomes the slut, the slag, the whore, the scrubber and so on. There are no comparable derogatory terms for males.

At the institutional level our legal system still epitomises our double standards, imposing greater control over female sexual behaviour than male and, in effect, punishing women and girls for behaviour overlooked in men and boys. Smith and Wilson (in this volume) deal with these issues in depth; it is sufficient to state here that the legal system is not impartial in its treatment of female 'offenders', and that the law itself embraces discriminatory standards (see Sachs, this volume; Chesney-Lind, 1973; Smart, 1976).

SUBORDINATE LEGAL AND SOCIAL STATUS

Women's legal and social status within the family is not equal to that of men. Socially, the housewife is not a prestigeous person within the community, her work is denigrated and there is very little public recognition of her value to the rest of society, as she is generally regarded as an unproductive worker. Her lack of social status is underpinned by her anomalous position in respect of legal and civil rights. On marriage a woman sacrifices many rights that a man does not. Legally, she has no protection from rape by her husband and the law protecting her from violent assault by her spouse is manifestly inadequate.(4) Even where the married woman works and pays a full National Insurance stamp, she is not entitled to the same unemployment benefit as a man (or a single woman) and she has no rights at all to social security benefits while unemployed. Even where she is single her rights to benefits are forfeited if she is believed to be co-habiting with a man (see Coote and Gill, 1974).

A woman does not have to be married to find herself differentially treated under our system of welfare provision. Many single women who have given up careers to look after old or infirm relatives have found they suffer a severe loss of benefits, while as a category, unmarried mothers constitute the poorest and most deprived section of our community because of inadequate state provision, minimal child-care facilities and low wages. The Welfare State operates with a conception of women which places them within the home, with children, with a man to support them; that this is not a reality for a great many women (e.g., the divorced, separated, widowed, working-married and single women) is ignored. Because of this false conception the Welfare State actually serves to perpetuate women's subordinate status within the family, promoting their economic and social dependence on men (Wilson, 1974; Land, 1976).

SEPARATION OF HOME AND WORK

The distinction between work and home, the public and the private,
is grounded in the structure of capitalist society. The development
of the capitalist mode of production required the socialisation of
the basic processes of commodity production, the development of
large-scale factory production and work outside the home. As
Zaretsky has succinctly stated: 'With the rise of industry, capitalism 'split' material production between its socialised forms (the
sphere of commodity production) and the private labour performed
predominantly by women within the home' (1976, p.29). This is the
origin of the distinction between the public and the private, between
work and personal life. The consequence for women of this separation
is that their work, domestic labour, has been consistently deprec-
iated within the community, the economy and the political system.
The traditional tasks of housework and child-rearing have not been
considered in relation to production because they do not represent a
source of surplus value. The division between home and work has had
a further consequence for women in that it has given rise to the
belief in a 'woman's place' being in the home rather than in the
world of work and production; this, despite the fact that in reality
many women are engaged in both housework (and the reproduction of
labour power) and wage labour. The ideology of women's place being
in the home has served to perpetuate the existing sexual division of
labour and to effectively limit the forms of women's participation
in the public domain (e.g., part-time, short-term or 'temporary'
employment), making a withdrawal into, and a predominant pre-
occupation with, or concern for, the home and family seem natural for
women.
   As we have attempted to show, the social control of women is a
complex phenomenon with many different dimensions, some of which are
explored in this collection of papers. The papers concentrate on
such neglected topics as the position, status and treatment of women
and girls in the areas of crime and delinquency, sexual promiscuity
and prostitution, and the discriminatory practices of the law and of
the legal and medical professions, offering critiques of the ideological and material conditions which control women and perpetuate their
oppression. Such analyses revealing the complex and concealed forms
of oppression and social control to which women are subject are
vital, for although explicit discrimination is now less socially
acceptable, and legislation has been passed which addresses some of
the more *overt* forms of exploitation and discrimination, the position,
status and material conditions of women have in many significant
respects remained virtually unchanged. It is to the analysis of such
issues that the papers in this volume are a contribution.

NOTES

1 See 'People', vol.2, no.2, 1975, a special International Women's
   Year issue containing articles on the position of women, legis-
   lation, etc. all over the world.
2 This formulation of women's oppression appears in Betty Friedan's
   'The Feminine Mystique' (1972), and derivatively in Sheila
   Rowbotham's 'Woman's Consciousness, Man's World' (1973).

3   On the male-dominated scientific control of contraception and
    abortion see Rose and Hanmer (1976), and Greenwood and Young
    (1976) respectively.
4   See M. Kemp et al (1975), and the 'Report from the Select
    Committee on Violence in Marriage'.

1 The coercion of privacy
A feminist perspective

Tove Stang Dahl and Annika Snare

INTRODUCTION

Our task in this paper is to outline and discuss a model for the
study of the structural coercion of women. Few women make it to the
privileged economic and political positions in society and there are
few of us among the outcasts in prisons. Women are thus publicly
less visible than men, and our rights, duties and crises are to a
larger degree individualised and privatised. The notion of *privacy*
is therefore of paramount importance, and its content, form and
consequence are our present concern.

After a brief review of traditional approaches to the question of
women, crime, deviance and social control, we will examine structural
means of coercion as they affect women's lives. Through the attempt
to conceptualise the nature of privacy, it should be possible to
better understand women's low participation in 'criminal life'.

Simultaneously such a perspective deals with how women's needs
lack protection by the law. This is a broad subject which can not be
covered in its entirety in this article. The myth of the law as
protector of a woman's integrity is revealed in most rape cases, but
the absence of criminal legislation to respond to harmful acts, such
as production of unsafe birth-control devices, medical experimenta-
tion on women, consumer frauds and so on, is as yet a fairly unexplored field.

By concentrating on legal *non-intervention* in the private sector,
we speak to the issue of economic injustice while at the same time
the role of primary, as opposed to secondary social control, is
analysed in a new light.

REVIEW

The issues discussed in this article generally fall outside the
traditional field of criminology. However, as a starting point a
few conventional comments on women and crime are in order. Using
official crime statistics, Norwegian women present themselves as
non-criminal in comparison to men. Historically over the last
hundred years the proportion of reported female criminality has

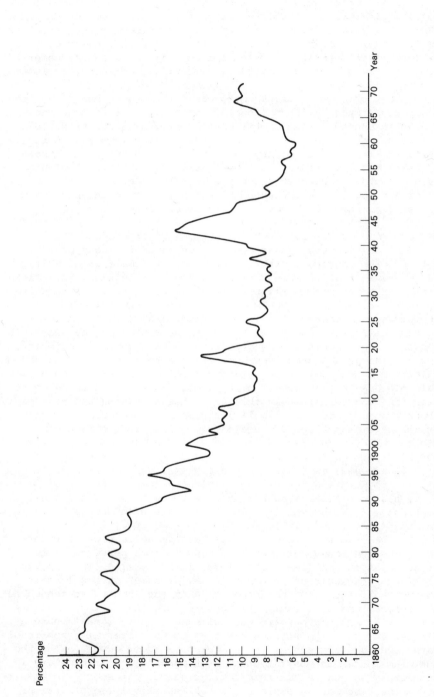

Figure 1   Percentage of reported crimes committed by women, 1860–1971 (Norwegian Official Criminal Statistics)

been declining with the notable exceptions of the two World Wars
(Table 1). In the early 1860s a comparatively high rate of 23 per
cent of all reported crimes were committed by women, but by the late
1950s the female proportion of registered criminality was reduced to
6 per cent (Enstad et al., 1974). This drastic decline was chiefly
a result of the decriminalisation of some sexual offences attributed
to women.

In current crime statistics women constitute less than 12 per cent
of all charges made by the police and not even 3 per cent of those
sentenced to unconditional imprisonment (criminal statistics, 1974)
(1). Approximately thirty women are incarcerated in Norway's female
correctional institution on any one day during the year. Furthermore, even this low figure might be considered 'artificially' high
compared to other countries since the overall female (as well as
male) prison population includes a large number of drunken drivers
sentenced to a three-week period of incarceration.

There is a controversy over the question as to why women commit
crimes or, more specifically, certain types of offences. The 'good-
evil woman' distinction and an emphasis on sexuality have predomin-
ated in studies concerned with the etiology of female criminality.
But a low rate of officially designated female criminals and a faster
declining proportion compared to male offenders at each consecutive
stage in the criminal justice system has raised the following
question: why are there so *few* female criminals?

Various different hypotheses have been presented in the search for
an answer to this question, ranging from women's moral superiority,
biological and psychological sex-differences to more encompassing
speculations on the impact of sex-role models. In certain countries,
notably the USA, crimes committed by women are reported to be on the
increase and not surprisingly this trend has attracted the mass media
and both academic and social-policy research. A recent addition to
the range of explanations of female criminality is the focus on a
possible link between women's liberation struggles and the increased
number of crimes committed by women. In particular, the focus has
been on an alleged new violent breed of female criminals (see Adler,
1975). The hypothesis concerning 'liberated female criminals',
however, has been criticised both on the basis of its ideological
assumptions *and* on an empirical level (see Klein and Kress, 1976;
Simon, 1975; Weis, 1976).(2)

Still, the main feature of the sparse criminological literature on
women is the continued reliance on a *pathological* perspective as
developed by Lombroso (see Klein, 1973; Smart, 1977). The 'status
quo' orientation inherent in much positivist thinking has largely
dominated the field, and characteristically the result has tended to
be ahistorical and individualistic interpretations. Simultaneously
certain sexist assumptions are made with respect to women's nature
in general and these postulates are treated as universally applicable
notwithstanding different class and cultural backgrounds. Thus the
common denominator in most hypotheses on women's low criminality is
the concern with sex rather than socio-economic sex-specified differences as the base for an explanation. Alternatively, explanations
have been sought in the criminal justice system itself by placing
great emphasis on the so-called chivalry of the male controllers
(Anderson, 1976). Once again this explanation of low rates of female

criminality in terms of a supposed discrimination in favour of women,
a supposition much revered and celebrated in the legal system and
criminological literature, is treated as a culturally universal
phenomenon benefiting all women independently of their class or
race.

The point is that in traditional research on women, deviation from
socially and legally accepted norms has persistently been treated on
the basis of male premises. Accordingly, female deviance, in contrast to male deviance, is explained in criminological textbooks in
terms of sexual characteristics of a biological or psychological
nature. To a certain extent, it is amazing that while male criminals and deviants in recent years have been studied from a sociological (including interactionist) position, this theoretical development has had little influence with regard to the study of female
illegal behaviour. Even the new/critical/radical criminology has not
paid much attention to the question of women and crime (we might add
that whether this is good or bad is another question). The reason for
this overall lack of interest is closely related to the crime
figures which were mentioned earlier. The few female criminals have
not caused alarm in the criminal justice system or among policy-
makers. In turn, neither agency-determined nor 'academic' research
has shown much interest in this subsidiary or residual category.

Most strikingly, not until the emergence of the current Women's
Movement has there been any distinct effort to structurally analyse
women's place in connection with the issues of deviance, criminality,
and social control. But in order to understand female deviant
behaviour, and in particular the low official crime activity of
women, it is necessary to focus on women's material conditions and
living situations as the point of departure. The importance of
developing a contextual framework on women's premises has to be seen
against the background of the vulgarisation of theory building which
has been so common in research on women's crime and deviance. As
alluded to before, it has been fully acceptable to use common-sense
sexist opinions as the foundation for non-critical empirical findings
(see Smart, 1976; Millman, 1975).

PERSPECTIVE

With regard to the criminology of women, the time has come for a
shift in paradigms and for a move away from the use of science in
the service of prejudice and oppression. The first issue is to find
a language in which women's experiences can be communicated and
understood in a societal perspective. The orienting points are
biography, history and society, or stated differently, a special
quality of mind - the sociological imagination. As C. Wright Mills
expressed it: 'The sociological imagination enables us to grasp
history and biography and the relationships between the two within
society. That is its task and its promise' (1959, p.6).

This formulation, the linking of the personal to the political,
and subjectivity to history, is well in accordance with recent
developments in the Norwegian Women's Movement. With reference to
the structural means of coercion vis-à-vis women such an approach
leads beyond the limits of the criminological field as it is usually

perceived.   In challenging traditional disciplinary boundaries, historical knowledge, as well as critical legal theory, can be of assistance.(3)

As a discipline, critical legal theory explores the way the law is grounded in the social structure, and based on this analysis it discloses the laws' ideological and legitimating character.   The focus is on the class nature of the legal system; how the law is bound to bourgeois interests and ultimately related to the existing mode of production.(4)   Moreover, a central feature in this analysis is the construction of *concepts* in order to be able to judge the current legal order.   Hence conceptualisation in the critical theory of law is derived directly from the actual objective and subjective conditions in an historically given society, in contrast to the ahistorical and abstract foundation as exemplified by the 'natural order' school of legal thought.   Again, we are back to the import-ance of an historical-sociological perspective in which the 'present' is documented as history.

It is the development of critical concepts to which we must first turn our attention.   For us the point of departure is the notion of privacy and its socio-political consequences.   The specific focus is the relegation of women into the private sector, a sector which is characterised by low public visibility and low mobility.   Further-more, within this household sphere, norms, conflicts and control mechanisms are personalised.   However, this notion of a 'private sphere' implies a false distinction between the problems of private life or personal troubles and public issues linked to the social structure.   The adoption of a critical stance towards the law promises to reveal the devices whereby women's needs and interests are translated into legal categories - abstract and often value-neutral concepts - which mask the nature of oppression which women experience.   The essential conditions of women's work and lives may be emphasised by making a comparison with an historical form of servitude.   The history in this case is not merely a 'general back-ground' but intrinsic to an understanding of the coercion of privacy.

In short, the intention is to present a *method* for the comprehen-sion of women's deviant or criminal behaviour as well as 'normal' behaviour by delineating the contours of the structural means of coercion and outlining the significance of the role played by these in the perpetuation of the existing order.   This proposed shift from an etiological concern with female offenders to a model analysing the relationship between women's current socio-legal status and the repressive state apparatus needs a continuing reappraisal and requires the integration of a feminist paradigm with a class analy-sis.   This 'dual' approach transcends the prevailing class-biased and male-dominated social science orientation, the goal being not only description and understanding but also fundamental social change.

THE PRIVATE SECTOR AND THE
'INVISIBILITY' OF WOMEN

The distinction between the 'private' and the 'public' sector has a material base and this division influences all areas of ordinary life.   Through their bonds to the institution of the family, women are primarily relegated to the private sector; on the other hand, men spend much of their life in paid production, working outside the domestic sphere in the public sector. Working outside the home a woman with a family is frequently considered to be engaged in a temporary and non-essential activity, an activity that is secondary to her domestic labour. In general, any one of the increasing number of women entering the workforce (by choice or material necessity) is regarded as belonging to the reserve labour pool. She carries a marginal labour status as reflected in insecure employment contracts and low wages. But specifically the notion prevails that the married woman's paid employment is of a supplementary nature and she usually continues to carry the home responsibilities. With or without such double work women's participation in any activities of the public section is low. They do not 'belong' there and in regard to the labour market women are considered transient.

In turn, domestic work and wage labour have distinctly different degrees of *visibility*. By being in the private sector women's social contributions, needs and problems are relatively invisible. Housekeeping is not considered the basis for estimating the level of national production and economic theories take little account of the kind of labour that women provide in society.(5) Moreover, domestic work is only to a minimum degree regulated by law and, in fact, is often forgotten in public policies. We will return to these two points after considering an exception to the lack of official attention paid to home production. This exception is the 'Kinder-Küche' role which receives hegemonic glorification. But this ideological visibility has not advanced women's emancipation, rather the real socio-economic position of women has been veiled and exempted from public scrutiny. The general privacy of the domestic household is a form of cover-up making for the preservation of the 'status quo', for what is invisible is extremely difficult to change.

In attempts to criticise and reject the idea that existing differences between the sexes constitute a 'natural order of things', the socialisation of young women into traditional sex-roles has been fairly well researched. However, less attention has been devoted to the judicial ideology which mystifies women's social reality and thereby reinforces and legitimises the hidden oppressive character of their lives. The legal rule of the protection of private life is a prime example of such an instrument. In discussing family crises we will look specifically at this issue. But the law's principle of non-intervention can also be viewed from another perspective which illustrates how the invisibility of women's activity serves to maintain existing social arrangements.

In the first Norwegian proposal (1975) for an equal rights amendment between the sexes, 'private life' was excluded from the projected policies, despite the fact that it is in this sector that the subordination of women is most prominent. Later, after pressure from the Women's Movement, 'private life' was incorporated within the proposed legislation; however this was a hollow victory for family life was designated as beyond the enforcement of the law (Dahl et al., 1975, 33).

The Equal Rights Bill shows in yet a second way the legal oppression of women. This time in the name of liberation. Indeed, women's *real* conditions are made invisible by legislative moves focusing on

formal equality. This distinction between real and formal rights is
crucial. In the Scandinavian countries the traditional judicial
discrimination against women has been almost completely eradicated.
Laws are now basically not sex-specified, they are *neutral,* but this
formal recognition of the equality of all citizens obscures discriminatory structures which in effect continue to exist, and this
situation requires judicial reforms providing *discrimination in
favour* of women.

The principle of formal equality and the principle protecting
privacy both function to uphold unequal social relations. Both are
coercive ideological forms which in Scandinavia at the present time
hinder women's liberation struggles. Loud protests against the equal
rights proposal indicate that Norwegian women no longer are content
with legal paternalism. Law reforms have to be accompanied by a
'delivery system' which in essence means a political and economic
reorganisation of society.

In summary, women's place in the private sector has briefly been
explored, the primary reference being the ideological context, the
focus being on the relationship between privacy and invisibility.
Lastly, we have argued that neutral laws are also a part of women's
hidden social reality. In the next section we take the analysis a
stage further, the material framework of women's and men's location
in different sectors is presented as it is reflected in the marriage
and the wage contract. These arrangements are two different sources
of economic support. The welfare system as a third sex-differentia-
ting possible source of survival is also discussed.

SOURCES OF LIVELIHOOD

From a societal viewpoint the distinction between home and wage
labour is an economic and sex-specified division of labour. From
an individual perspective, the issue is one of different sources of
survival. The primary source of livelihood for men is the wage
contract, while for females the marriage contract plays a similar
role. The similarity between the two arrangements is succinctly
expressed below:
    Marriage is a contract which is theoretically entered into freely
    by a man and a woman. However, for the woman there is little
    choice involved - they may choose whom to marry, but they will
    not willingly remain unmarried. An analogy may be useful.
    Members of the working class may choose their employers, but they
    will not remain unemployed if they can help it, and they cannot
    be independent since they own no capital. (Quick, 1972, p.3).
A third source of livelihood is welfare measures such as unemployment insurance, sick and old-age pensions and the like. This
alternative is highly developed in the Welfare State but welfare
provisions differ for women and men. Most people move between the
three possible sources of subsistence: income, marriage and social
security. Some are in all three at the same time; the main source,
however, is constantly related to the variables sex, age and health.

Moreover, due to the predominance of men in the labour market,
they have without doubt a much more assured legal status with regard
to public assistance than women. In order to acquire a right to

many of the welfare benefits, an individual has to be a constituent
of wage-labour power. As clarified before, most women are merely a
reserve work-force dependent on market forces or the economic trend,
and thereby do not obtain independent rights to this economic basis
of survival. Besides, cultural hegemony underlines the assumption
that women's 'true' method of life support is the husband.

In most cases welfare policies are based on the assumption that
women have and indeed are supposed to have a private supporter.
This economic guarantee sometimes allows for the firing of women
when the labour market needs to discharge workers (Finstad, 1975).
Thus women's marginal labour position and their assumed private
means of support make them likely to be fired, since men as the
primary breadwinners would have to be more thoroughly taken care of
by the public support system. Once again the rules are formed in
such a way as to pressure women into the private sector.

Women's borderline status in paid employment and in the social
security system becomes clearer when one looks at the living situation of widows or single mothers. They do acquire independent
economic rights through law, but only as long as no private
supporter is present. The two other sources of survival, income
or welfare are *subsidiary* to the main one, but not equally favoured
by the State. A widow obtains financial assistance to become self-
sufficient as a wage earner. This means that at a time when she is
left alone with children and home, she is guided into the work-
force. On the other hand, as long as she was privately provided
for and maybe had the strength and wish to find outside employment,
nothing was done to help her. The right to paid work only appears
when she is a burden to the State's budget.

Separated, divorced and unmarried mothers experience a similar
process of expulsion from the welfare system to paid employment.
Although, in these instances the welfare policies are particularly
directed towards 'encouraging' women into the institution of private
provision. The law sees to it that a single mother loses her right
to public support if she lives with the father of the child (or a
presumed father). Intervening practice by social agencies is even
stricter. Both in Norway and Denmark, unmarried mothers are not
allowed to live with any man if they are to keep their acquired
welfare status. Thus the State promotes the traditional family
institution but condemns its 'illegal' counterpart if the woman with
her limited earning power has to rely on public support. The kind
of control which is carried out by the authorities is hardly in
accordance with the sacred principle of privacy. This legal doc-
trine is foremost attached to the nuclear family arrangement, and
one may be justified in proposing that the protection of the private
life of the man has been the chief concern of the law. As a side
comment in this matter, it is ironic to note that in the case of
women's control of their *own* bodies, the law has readily interfered.
For example, abortion is not regarded as a woman's personal decision
but as a public (i.e. male) issue.(6)

The development of the two sexes' separate main sources of
material survival is historically rooted in the advancement of
industrial capitalism. In time the 'free' wage contract absorbed a
progressively larger proportion of the male population. In an early
phase of the establishment of a new political economy, women's

labour was also demanded. However, by and large women have only
been integrated into the money market on a dependent basis. Hence
they participate through the function of the family as a centre of
consumption or partly through being a supplementary labour commodity - the second-best team in the dual labour market of industrial
capitalist production.

The conclusion is that women are situated in a dependent relationship to male supporters. Labour, welfare and family legislation
preserves the prevailing conditions of a women's livelihood. To be
outside paid employment has two consequences which are of a special
importance in exploring coercive forces in women's lives. One
factor is simply *the lack of cash*. The marriage contract gives
many of its benefits in goods and therefore women often only have
small and insecure sums of money at their disposal. In this
matter potential welfare rights are not of much help. Married
women in Norway under the age of 67 who are not working outside
the home, have at their own independent disposal basically *only*
the public child allowance.(7)

Second, women in the private sector are severely restricted in
their mobility both because of their specific family duties and, as
a consequence, their lack of money. The concept of *immobility* is
thus embodied in the nuclear family and in the marriage contract.
An analogy can serve us in the investigation of *housewife servitude*.

A FEUDAL LEGACY

There are apparent similarities between the predominant form of work
arrangement flourishing in the eighteenth and nineteenth centuries
and the current marriage system. Before the introduction of 'free'
labour contracts, the working situation of the rural labouring poor
was regulated by master-servant rules.(8)   Even though the arrangement legally was a voluntary partnership, the form of the contract
and the character of the work relation was closely connected to the
employer's offer. The servant or *'houseman'* (as the farming
labourer or cottier was called in Norway) was subjected to an
obligation to work and a duty to settle in the master's lodgings.
The salary consisted mainly of goods rather than money, and the
amount or quality of payment did not vary directly with the work
contribution but varied instead with the status and attitude of the
farmer in question. The servant's working hours were not stipulated
by law. He had an 'unspecified and unconditional' work obligation
and expected to labour whenever he was commanded to do so.

These 'housemen' were not allowed to have side-line employment
without the master's permission. The mobility of the employee was
generally severely restricted and his position after being fired was
weak. If the 'houseman' became of age at the time of unemployment,
he was in an especially powerless situation. (Regarding this point
a comparison with the housewife seems superfluous.) Viewed broadly
the relationship between the master and the servant created a mutual
dependency where the latter's dependent status was closely linked to
the benevolence of his superior.

In many ways today's housewife is in the same subordinate position as the 'houseman' of past times. The duty to work is assumed

in the marriage contract and the settlement required is contained in
the nature of household labour. The housewife has no regulated work
time but is supposed to be 'on duty' all day long and during all
seasons. She has little chance of moving around and is to a
large degree dependent on the husband's consent when it comes to
employment and leisure activities. In addition a common feature of
the past and present form of servitude is the lack of organised
political action for improving working conditions. Not until the
break-up of the traditional labour bonds, did strikes become a
viable alternative. Similarly, except for the all-women 'walk out'
in Iceland in 1975, housewives have so far not organised a collective strike.

The housewife is thus placed in a quasi-feudal work arrangement
outside the money economy (see also Bengtsson, 1969). Apart from the
physical reproduction of new members of the labour force, her tasks
are manifold in the arena of home duties. Use value is created by
women's production of goods and services. From a political and
economic viewpoint the end product within the household realm is
the creation of new workers and the maintenance (reparative work) of
those who constitute the present work-force. On an individual basis
the psychological contribution in the form of emotional support and
comfort to today's and the future's labourers should not be under-
estimated, not the least since women themselves place so much
emphasis on their private responsibility in this critical area.

The housewife's dependency on her 'master' is of a material as
well as personal character. Both his class status and individual
attitudes are significant features. The content of the master-
servant contract was, and the content of the marriage contract is,
characterised by its individualised and privatised nature. The
happy 'houseman' arrangement has its counterpart in the mutually
satisfactory marriage. But the essential foundation is a feudal
structure in which a paternalist ideology rules in order to sustain
the prevailing power hierarchy.

RIGHTS

The growth of capitalism caused the dissolution of feudal types of
labour bonds and the creation of other exploitative work relations.
The housewife, however, remains in servitude. The legal structure
around the contemporary family institution illustrates this statement. More to the point, the lack of legislation with regard to
home production reinforces the existing privatised arrangement. As
in the case of 'neutral laws', the significant factor is not so much
what the law says but what it defines as outside the limits of its
jurisdiction.

Norwegian law has few regulations concerning the private sphere.
The mutual duty to provide for the family is stipulated in the first
paragraph of the Marriage Act, but there is quite an omnipresent
lack of independent rights for the one who has the responsibility
for home production (unless the contract is broken through separation and divorce). For example, if the wife does not have additional paid work outside the family her insurance rights are weak. She
has no right to monetary assistance in times of sickness, only a

right to hospitalisation and medical help. In the case of disability the housewife does have an economic right of her own, but the
requirements are strict while at the same time the insurance is
small and easily rescinded (cf. Højer, 1974). Additionally, when
a housewife attempts to find employment in a closed labour market
she cannot obtain unemployment status since this right is tied to
the applicant's former work activity as a wage earner. In this
respect it is interesting to note in passing that military service
as a contribution to society is valued both in connection to unemployment and other social insurances.

It is difficult not to reach the conclusion that married men
appropriate the economic benefits acquired through the division of
labour within the family institution. The husband's financial
situation clearly deteriorates if he must rely on a paid housekeeper instead of a wife; apart from the housekeeper's salary,
national insurance and other expenses also have to be paid to the
State. But if the man marries the housekeeper economic advantages
follow since the law implicitly regards cash payments within
marriage as support and not remuneration for work done. Income-tax
regulations represent an additional specific obstruction, keeping
Norwegian women from attempting to find employment (see Zimmer,
1975).

Public insurance regulations also give the husband additional
financial rights through the wife's domestic labour since payments
are sometimes made directly to him. To re-emphasise the point, up
until the time she is eligible for an old-age pension, the public
child support is the only cash the housewife/mother can uncon-
ditionally demand; there is no discretionary judgment and the money
is given directly to her. Admittedly, this is an indirect claim
acquired through the child, but it functions as an independent
right based on mothers' real responsibilities.

Marriage gives women few legal economic claims and in those areas
where her contribution in the home leads to certain rights, the
rules are formulated in such a way that the man, as the head of the
household, administers the public support even if it originates from
the woman's work. Accordingly the 'household law' entitles its pro-
ducer to meagre monetarial rights while simultaneously the wife has
no control over the husband's income and therefore is at his mercy
for household money.

Economic theories as well as legislative doctrines treat the
family as a private economic unit and avoid the fact that opposite
interests might exist *within* the same entity. Fundamentally, the
housewife's legal position is a reflection of the husband's. Apart
from the necessary requirements with respect to entering and dis-
closing a marriage, the law does not intervene. Conflicts between
the partners are not legally acknowledged; the family institution
is supposed to function in harmony after the contract is signed and
until the relationship has possibly deteriorated to the extent that
a disclosure is necessary.

This *consensus* model stands in sharp contrast to much of existing
family reality. The practice of non-intervention when conflicts
occur in the private sector should constitute a significant topic
for criminological investigation.

CONFLICTS AND CRISES

For many women the marital arrangement signifies a life of economic,
psychological and physical dependency on a man. 'Breaking-up' is
difficult due to the labour market situation and the material as
well as emotional barriers of the bond. Even escape from the violent excesses within the family sphere is a burdensome matter.
Physical acts of cruelty such as wife-battering and rape are not
uncommon. Yet following the sacred principle of privacy, the act of
rape by a husband against the wife is in many countries judicially
impossible. In Norway the wife's personal integrity has been confirmed through a Supreme Court decision in 1974 admitting that rape
within marriage can occur, and thereby acknowledging that there are
some limits to the sexual rights a husband has over 'his' wife.

Despite this legal precedent, the wife's protection by the law
against physical abuses is nevertheless much weaker than if she had
not been married to the man in question. The court cases of rape
within marriage and wife-battering are few in number. There are
issues of evidential proof, and defence declarations claiming pro-
vocations by the wife are easily obtained: any rape victim has to
'prove' that she did not seduce the man and the abused wife is often
regarded as having provoked the husband into beating her.(9)

The judicial obstacle towards conviction is preceded by the
police and social authorities' inability or unwillingness to intervene in family disputes even when it is evident that the violence
is both extensive and life threatening. Despite the lack of public
attention, surveys - mostly from countries outside of Scandinavia -
have revealed a much greater frequency of wife-battering than was
previously supposed.(10) It has also been shown how representatives
of the police, welfare and health agencies do not offer adequate
support in these often repetitive ordeals of domestic brutality (see
Pizzey, 1974).

These acts of domination remain invisible. The indifference of
the legal system to women's need for protection is partly a
result of scepticism regarding the 'worthiness' of the victim.
However, women themselves will also often prefer to not press
charges against their husbands and bring 'internal' conflicts to
court. This attitude should be viewed as a reflection of both the
victim's bondage to the economic basis of her life-support and of
social indoctrination which transforms the beatings into a personal
failure. Marital violence is thus seen by women as shameful - or as
their own fault - all of which makes it embarrassing and degrading
to seek help.

Restricted in their mobility and lacking financial resources,
abused wives often have nowhere to turn for assistance. One way to
ameliorate the situation has been the establishment of refuges where
women and children can receive immediate shelter as well as emotional
counselling.(11) Shelters, counselling and law enforcement are
necessary components against the physically coercive force of rape
and wife-abuse. Marital brutality has to be approached as a public
issue rather than an individual problem. In support of this strategy it can be mentioned that wife-battering has been incorrectly
assumed to be only a working-class phenomenon. Upper- and middle-
class women might be especially reluctant to consider, for example,

calling the police, or they may use alternative means, not available
to working-class women, to break away from brutality in the family.
Although the issue as to the extent of wife-beating in different
classes is still not clear, there is evidence to show that the crime
is not confined to any one class; it mirrors the pattern of sexual
domination prevalent in all social relationships between the sexes.

Family members' disapproval of turning to external methods of
social control, welfare agencies' non-response and battered women's
lack of perception of themselves as a collectively abused group has
veiled the magnitude of domestic violence. Moreover, men in power
define and enforce definitions, therefore, in line with their interests, wife-battering has not been regarded as a social problem.
Communication between victims and the growth of pressure-group
support has provided the impetus for a redefinition of the problem
from an individual concern to a societal issue.

The privatisation of a social problem such as wife-abuse is not a
single isolated phenomenon in the private sector. Rather women's
problems are generally viewed as personal difficulties appropriately
solved through *private reactions*. For example, when despite its
calm surface, pressures are building up within the family, the
stress condition is experienced and treated as an individual
dilemma. Both persons involved and outsiders neglect the social
aspect of the crisis and therefore a public issue is defined as
only a personal concern. Consequently attempts at a solution are
individualised. It is worth noting that the medical profession
plays an important role in emphasising and strengthening this
privatisation, e.g., women's utilisation of medication such as
tranquillisers is more extensive than men's and the use increases
with the degree of economic and cultural poverty (see Christie,
1976).

With regard to medication the socio-political as opposed to
personal nature of drug use is revealed by the fact that the usage
is correlated to the husband's work hours and rises when he works
in shifts. The wife's stress is aggravated when the demand for
consideration, self-sacrifice and self-effacement reaches the
borderline of the family's endurance. If her threshold is reached,
hospitalisation is the next step. Available evidence from existing
investigations point to the fact that more women than men are
institutionalised in mental hospitals. Clearly, more research is
needed on statistical trends of psychiatric confinement according
to sex and other variables. As it now stands, a larger number of
women than men appear to be in Danish institutions while the
opposite seems to be true in Norwegian ones. However, as elsewhere, in Norway the proportion of women in mental hospitals is
much higher than in prisons.(12)

In the case of the 'maladjusted' woman societal reaction takes
the form of treatment and hospitalisation. The sex-specified control syndrome has been summarised in the following way:

Women solve their problem in a legally accepted way using the
pharmacy as their source. The medication perhaps becomes a kind
of lubrication, a method to keep these women or to make these
women keep themselves functioning - just at the level they do
function. (Christie, 1976, p.74)

Women's problems are, then, not visible. Interestingly enough, the

use of alcohol (which so far has been predominantly a male pattern)
is more easily detected by others and thereby open to official
reaction by the criminal justice system. In contrast, the use of
tranquillisers is a concealed approach to a stress condition and a
more privatised strategy of control. As a fearful example of the
private and public utility of invisible mechanisms of social control, the quotation from a newspaper below hardly needs any further
comment:

HOSPITALIZED - WITHOUT THE FAMILY NOTICING ANYTHING

I can only praise the day-care provided al Ulleval (a hospital
in Oslo). My family does not notice that I am hospitalized. My
husband and children leave the house at the same time in the
morning as I do, and I am back before them and have dinner ready
by the time they arrive. (Christie, 1976, p.76)

Physically and emotionally isolated women tend towards a conservative personalisation of the world. This view is reinforced by
informal means of control such as the use of medical drugs in controlling errant and troubled women. Their needs for self-fulfilment,
their struggles with low self-esteem and social problems are hidden
from view and therefore fail to receive the attention they deserve
or their share of critical publicity and study in much the same way
as the family itself is forgotten by the law and official policy.
The coercion of privacy restrains women to the extent that we might
speak of them living their lives in a private prison. This perspective offers an understanding of women's exceptionally low involvement with the criminal justice system.

THE PRIVATE PRISON

Some women commit acts which lead to interference by the legal
system. An offence like shoplifting is closely linked to women's
consumer function in the private sector. Young women are frequently
apprehended because of their involvement in narcotics related
crimes. The illegal use of drugs is condemned by the State while
its legal equivalent is approved. Either usage, however, is an
individualised and privatised act in accordance with the female
pattern of deviant and criminal behaviour.

Drug addicts in the black market are formally punished and they,
together with other 'serious' female offenders, are imprisoned. But
only a few women are incarcerated in a public prison. On a quantit-
ative basis many more women are controlled through informal methods.
A woman's seclusion fosters close control by children, husband and
neighbours. Sociologically speaking the dominant tool is primary
rather than secondary social control.

Among students of sociology there is a certain tendency to
glorify earlier historical periods when family and peer group relations supposedly regulated people's lives. This romantic notion is
then juxtaposed to today's formal bureaucratic organisation of State
control. Undoubtedly, State intervention has increased in a number
of specific social areas (for example health and education) since
the late nineteenth century. (13) However, despite the growth in the
formal control apparatus women are largely controlled through

informal means. Furthermore, the kind of primary control which
affects women in the private sector has a distinctly coercive trait.
Linked to the close supervision women experience is the legal conception of the sacred character of private life and the non-
intervention practice of social agencies in cases of family violence and conflicts. Additionally, the powerless situation of women
is ideologically reinforced by academic disciplines which continue
to rely only on a consensus model in their approach to the marriage
contract and the household realm.

It is necessary to deal with the coercive impact of informal
means of control, with conflicting interests between wife and husband, and the 'status quo' effect of invisibility. Pragmatically,
women's right to money and mobility are of great concern as well.
From this standpoint we submit that on an ideological level (including many practical implications), the nuclear family represents
a prison comparable to the public institution carrying this label.
(14)

What does it mean to be a prisoner? Deprivation of liberty
signifies that one is declared incapable of managing one's own
affairs and therefore robbed of the power of self-determination.
Life in the public and private prison has many common institutional
features: the official penal institution deprives the prisoners of
their identity, prevents them from having 'their own places',
degrades their personality, and takes them 'out of circulation'.
By creating an authoritarian control system the prison constructs
a number of barriers in the form of physical restrictions of
mobility and in the form of restraints concerning social life.

Similarly it can be argued that women are segregated and locked
in their 'cells', the nuclear family, where they are hindered from
having their own personal life due to lack of mobility, cash and
free time. In particular a housewife with small children can not
regulate her own time. With the important qualification in mind
that in society at large loss of autonomy and choice are class-
bound factors, one can propose that through material and ideological bonds, women are kept 'out of circulation', if we mean by that
a life in the public sector where men (of the ruling class) are now
in control.

Both the official and the 'house' arrest are part of the total
social control apparatus. Clearly the link between the two institutions of confinement merits attention. The only Norwegian prison
for women - Bredtveidt - has aptly been unofficially labelled a
'housewife's school' (a domestic science school) and in regard to
the rehabilitative measures provided for the prisoners it promotes
an ideology which increases the pressure on women to gravitate
towards the traditional function for a woman of caretaker of the
family.(15) Individual adjustment of erring women to their 'natural'
feminine role becomes the key concern in the resocialisation process in institutions of this kind.

In responding to the question of why there are so few women who
are officially punished, our argument relies on the notion of a
private prison. It is not because the female sex is morally superior or women are socially strong enough to avoid interference by
the criminal justice system as could be argued in the case of high
status groups. Women are controlled through all the conditions -

structural means of coercion - that keep them oppressed in society.
Women are tied to their household sphere with its service demands
and locked out of paid production. Even when we participate in the
labour-force many of us are restricted by the double burden of wage
and domestic labour. This 'imprisonment' is ideologically
strengthened by women's lack of self-confidence, by myths, expectations, socialisation and so on. When something goes wrong in the
private prison, medical solutions are expedient. Similarly it can
be observed that within the public prison the use of drugs, chemo-
therapy, is becoming a standard managerial practice for ensuring
order and control. Privately imprisoned, only the most exposed
women are taken care of by the official control agencies and this
selection by the State follows the classist nature of the capitalist
legal system.

CONCLUSION

In Norway the most characteristic feature of Bredtveidt has been
the 'silence' surrounding the institution. Access for outsiders is
difficult to obtain and relatively little is publicly known about
the inside life of women ending up in prison.(16) This lack of
access to female prisons has also been noted in other countries.
However, in the case of male prisoners the situation is different,
for in recent years they have received public attention. Through
prisoners' rebellions and outside movements their plight and
demands have become visible in more than one country.
   The exposure of the conditions in women's prisons is a crucial
task if pressure is to be mounted for reforms which could offer the
prisoners opportunities to obtain satisfactory work, living conditions and other help necessary for them to be able to live a self-
determined life upon release. But if it is correct that large
numbers of women on the outside live their lives in dependency and
servitude, the private prison also has to be made visible. This
article represents an attempt in that direction. At the same time
we acknowledge that making the coercion of the private sphere
visible is only a very first step in the struggle towards the
elimination of an economic order which fosters sexism and the
oppression of both sexes.

NOTES

1 In 1974 women constituted 8.5 per cent of all offenders
   receiving some kind of penal sanction. In the same year a
   total of 98 women were sentenced to unconditional imprisonment
   for their offences. The major crime categories were: theft
   (39), public crimes, i.e. Narcotics (29), forgery (18) and
   violent crimes (9). In addition there were 82 imprisonments
   for drunken driving which in Norway is a misdemeanour which
   nearly always results in a prison sentence (Criminal Statistics,
   1974).
2 In Norway the recorded female crime rate rose from 6 per cent to
   11 per cent during the 1960s. Nils Christie (1975) attributed

this increase to more women participating in public life and in
the wage labour-force (an implicit 'liberation' argument). A
closer look at the statistics, however, reveals that most of
the increase was due to petty theft (shoplifting) and drug
offences. Neither of these crimes can justifiably be attributed
to female wage-earners. Second, when shoplifting was reduced
from a criminal offence to a misdemeanour (1972), the official
proportion of female criminality declined.

3 The present paper relies partly on an earlier version by Tove
   Stang Dahl on the legal system and the societal importance of
   control through privacy; see Dahl (1976a) for additional information on Norwegian law. For a discussion of critical legal
   theory in general and its Marxist foundation, see Eriksson
   (1976, pp.202-12).

4 In the German and East European Marxist-Leninist school of legal
   thought the law is rather mechanically treated on the basis of
   concepts derived from political economy (Eriksson, 1976).
   Through this purely deductive approach in the search for the
   'necessary' relationships between the economic base and the
   superstructure, women's struggle (as in the case of racial
   minorities) receives scanty consideration.

5 The Chase Manhattan Bank estimates the average American housewife's work-week to be 99.6 hours (Rowbotham, 1973). Literature
   on women's work includes Bengtsson (1969), Galbraith (1973) and
   Quick (1972). In Norway this debate is ongoing, for example,
   the journal 'Kjerringrad' dedicated one issue to the question of
   unpaid labour (no.5, 1976). In Italy and England there is an
   increasing movement (with branches in the USA) for wages for
   housework (see Dalla Costa and James, 1973; Edmond and Fleming,
   1975; Il Collettivo Internazionale Femminista, 1975).

6 A proposal on the right to free abortion was rejected by Parliament in 1974 (78 against 77 votes). Instead in Norway there
   were some changes in the law which in fact have not produced an
   improvement over earlier practice, indeed the enforcement of the
   new legislation has tended to put socially and geographically
   resourceless women in an especially weak position. The topic of
   legislation on sexuality is beyond the scope of the present
   project. However on female juvenile 'promiscuity' and the up-
   holding of ruling sexual norms by the courts, see Chesney-Lind
   (1973). There is a rather vast literature on prostitution and
   a shift towards viewing the prostitute as a victim in society,
   rather than an offender, has taken place, see Women Endorsing
   Decriminalization (1973).

   In Scandinavia prostitution as such is decriminalised and a
   vast amount of 'semi-prostitution' (for example, massage par-
   lours, escort services and pornography) is legalised. In
   Denmark where the porno-industry has been especially widespread,
   feminists have now begun to strongly attack a legal system
   which supports a capitalist patriarchal society's violence
   against women (see Report from the Danish Red Stockings Movement to the Brussel Tribunal on Crimes against Women, 4-8 March
   1976). The point to stress is that lack of legal rules does
   not reform the conditions of oppressed groups if the causes of
   the oppression are not eliminated.

7 A government income tax commission proposed in 1976 that the
   public child support should be divided between the mother and
   the father and partly incorporated as a tax deduction. This
   attempt to formally create equality would eliminate one of the
   few rights to money that women are at present ensured. The
   right to money is a crucial demand for women's liberation.
8 Historically different types of labour statutes prevailed in
   Europe. The Norwegian development of labourers' servitude is
   described by Skappel (1922) from whom the present account is
   taken.
9 The first Norwegian book on rape was published recently.
   Written by a feminist, it describes and analyses how most rape
   cases handled by the Oslo police never reach the courts, and
   even fewer rapists are ever convicted (Lykkjen, 1976). For an
   account of prevailing rape myths, see Schwendinger and
   Schwendinger (1974, pp.18-26).
10 An article in 'Ms.' (August 1976) entitled Most American
   Violence Happens in the Home states that there were 4,764
   reported rapes in New York State in 1973 (according to the FBI),
   while during a comparable period about 14,000 wife-abuse complaints reached the Family Courts. Although the USA might be
   the leading nation with regard to these violent crimes, the
   Norwegian police also intervene daily in cases labelled 'domestic disturbance'. Research is starting at the Institute of
   Criminology and Criminal Law (Oslo) to determine the extent
   and nature of marital abuse in these cases. On a more general
   level a study of victims of violence admitted to the emergency
   ward of an Oslo hospital indicates that women are beaten inside
   the home while men are involved in fights in public places
   (Lind, 1969).
11 The first in England - which has been the design for others -
   was Chiswick Women's Aid Centre. For the story of this refuge,
   see Pizzey (1974). There now exist around 50 refuges in
   England and the number is also growing in the USA. Ireland and
   Australia have established shelters, while France and Germany
   are in the developing phase ('Ms.', August 1976), so is Norway.
12 It should be taken into account that standards for mental
   health are sex-specified (Roth and Lerner, 1975). Women have
   long been 'ideal' mental patients and medical guinea pigs; the
   US 'father of psychosurgery' noted that women made the best
   candidates for lobotomy, and mentioned one elderly housewife who
   'was a master at bitching and really led her husband a dog's
   life' until surgery made her into a model housekeeper (cited in
   Klein and Kress, 1976, p.44). For an extensive discussion of
   women's mental health and the treatment they get, see Chesler
   (1972).
13 For a critical socio-historical analysis of extended state-
   involvement in the field of correction and education of children,
   see Dahl (1977).
14 At the Institute of Criminology and Criminal Law, Oslo, Liv
   Finstad is specifically exploring the similarities between
   female prisoners' conditions and women's oppression in the
   private prison. Her thinking has been helpful in this section.

15 The treatment offered by the prison authority might be consid-
    ered successful in the sense that female prisoners who fail to
    offend again are those who marry, have children and live in a
    stable marriage.
16 From official documents it is known that at the time of the
    creation of a special woman's prison (1881), practical economic
    concerns and not any direct considerations of female prisoners'
    welfare was the main factor (Thomassen et al., 1976). Today
    this neglected category still has low priority when it comes to
    planning and funding in the criminal justice system.

2 The myth of male protectiveness and the legal subordination of women
An historical analysis

Albie Sachs

One of the problems with which Victorian and Edwardian judges
wrestled for sixty years was whether or not women could in law be
regarded as 'persons'. The cases arose out of the use of the word
'person' in a number of statutes which dealt with qualifications
for holding public office, exercising the vote and entering the
professions. The issue was whether females otherwise qualified to
participate in these activities were debarred by virtue of the fact
that they were not 'persons', and in every case except the last (1)
the judges held that they were in fact so disqualified.(2) There
were other cases too in which the judges set their faces against
women's claims, the most notable being the exclusion of Sophia
Jex-Blake and other women from Edinburgh Medical School (on the
extraordinary grounds that the University Senate were entitled to
treat their own regulations authorising female entry as 'ultra
vires', 1874), the refusal of permission to Bertha Cave to read for
the Bar (1903), and the exclusion of Lady Rhondda from the House of
Lords (1922).

The purpose of this essay is to examine the conception of womanhood articulated in these cases as intellectual or moral justification for the legal decisions. The judges were fully aware that the
impact of their rulings was to deny to women opportunities to enter
the more lucrative occupations or to participate in public life
alongside men. But far from being defensive or apologetic, they
insisted that what they were doing was right, not only for society
but for the women concerned. Time and again the judges asserted
that they were not imposing disabilities based on inferiority, but
granting exemptions based on respect. They wrote with the ease of
upper-middle-class men confident in their world view and aware of
their special role as articulators of the official sense of justice
of their times. They assumed that men and women inhabited totally
different spheres, each with its own set of rights and duties. The
underlying principle was that the two sexes were neither the same
with regard to rights, nor even separate but equal, but, rather,
different and complementary.

The judges were ever quick to emphasise how deeply they respected women. They did not actually say that they counted women
amongst their best friends, but they were assiduous in their

emphasis on how 'courteous, tender and reverent' they felt towards
females. The words which constantly recur in describing their
attitudes towards women are decorum, respect and propriety. In
their view, this respect for women did not hold women back, but
shielded them from the harsh vicissitudes of public life. Male
judges and male legislators were at one in holding that male vener-
ation surrounded and upheld the delicacy of women, and, far from
debasing or oppressing women, elevated them to a superior position.
One Member of Parliament declared that a man would be ennobled by
possession of the vote, but a woman would be degraded by it, since
she would lose the admirable attributes of her sex, namely her
gentleness, affection and domesticity. In his opinion, and he
spoke as a lawyer, the very disabilities of women taken as a whole
showed how great a favourite the female sex was to the laws of
England.(3)
    The most striking aspect of the judicial and other pronouncements
on female delicacy is that what was asserted as incontrovertible
fact was in reality nothing more than fallacious abstraction. Very
few of the women whom the judges knew, whether they were litigants,
or cleaners of the courtroom, or servants in the home, actually
corresponded in any way to the judicial representation. At the
time when the judges were speaking, more than a million unmarried
women alone were employed in industry, while a further three-
quarters of a million women were in domestic service. The judges
had only to read the 'Edinburgh Review' to discover a 'horrifying'
analysis by an anonymous feminist of the nature, pay and conditions
of women's work.(4) For the great majority of Victorian women, as
for the great majority of Victorian men, life was characterised by
drudgery and poverty rather than by refinement and decorum.
Applying the judges' criteria, then, most women were simply not
women. And, if John Stuart Mill can be accepted, far from men being
the natural protectors of women, husbands battered their wives at
least as frequently as they do today. Mill told Parliament that he
should like to have a Return of the number of women who were
annually beaten, kicked or trampled to death by their male protectors, and to contrast the sentences imposed, if any, with the same
punishments by the same judges for thefts of small amounts of
property. 'We should then have an arithmetical estimate', he
declared, 'of the value set by a male legislature and male tribun-
als on the murder of a woman, often by torture continued through
years' (House of Commons Debates, 20 May 1867).
    The sexual myth in fact fitted in neatly in practical terms with
the myth of judicial neutrality, though logically they should have
been incompatible. In all the public rights cases except the last
one, the effect of the judgments was to deny the women's claims and
to maintain male supremacy. The judicial myth justified this on
the grounds that the judges were merely the impartial instruments
of the law precluded from investigating the desirability or otherwise of women being allowed to do the things they wished to do. The
sexual myth, on the other hand, justified the judgments on the
grounds that the exclusion of women from public life was a mark of
special respect rather than a sign of special disregard. Thus the
notions were simultaneously advanced that the judges were entirely
non-partisan and that the judges were protecting the women for their

own advantage. These apparently contradictory myths were reconciled
in intention if not in logic, since they both served the same end of
giving the appearance of justice to what otherwise would have been
manifest inequity.

The myth of male decorum was most strongly expressed by Judge
Willes in the Manchester Voters case and by most of the judges in
the Edinburgh Seven case. Willes was in fact one of the most
admired judges of his day, and his sentiments on women were singled
out for approbation by many judges during the next half century.
Responding to the claim by counsel for the women that to deny them
the vote purely on grounds of sex when they fulfilled all other
qualifications, was to hold that women were to be treated on a par
with imbeciles, he expressly protested against it being thought
that the legal incapacity of women arose from any underrating of the
sex either in point of intellect or of worth. That would be inconsistent, he declared, with one of the glories of civilisation - the
respect and honour in which women were held. In his view, the exclusion of women from public office was to be seen as an exemption
founded upon motives of decorum, and be regarded as a privilege
rather than a disability. The claims by Sophia Jex-Blake and her
colleagues at Edinburgh University Medical School that they should
in every way be treated on the same basis as men, aroused horror in
virtually all the judges, whose concepts of womanhood were grossly
offended by the notion of female students studying anatomy in mixed
classes, and, even worse, carving presumably nude cadavers in the
presence of male students. The more extreme anti-feminist view as
expressed by Lord Neaves was that women should be kept out of university altogether. He hastened to observe that women's powers were
as noble as those of men, only rather inferior when it came to
severe and incessant work; the weaker mental constitution of female
students would inevitably hold back the rest of the class, just as
the admission of women to the medical profession would threaten its
high standards. He noted further that the instruction necessary
for mastering household and family affairs, as well as the ornamental branches of education which aided social refinement and
domestic happiness, would distract from university studies, while
conversely the lack of feminine arts and attractions would hardly
be supplied by the sort of knowledge gained at a university. Women
would benefit from universities, he averred, but only indirectly
through having their fathers, brothers, husbands and sons better
educated.

The more sympathetic judicial view was that women could be
allowed to qualify as doctors, and yet not cause sexual embarrass-
ment, by means of attending separate classes. Lord Deas felt that
for a small group of women to be shut up with an overwhelming
majority of men would have caused the women such unease that they
might have felt a greater sense of grievance than they did at being
excluded altogether. For their own sake, therefore, it was a
reasonable policy to exclude them from mixed classes. Lord
Ardmillan, on the other hand, stressed that much as he admired
intelligent and virtuous women he could only be shocked by the
thought of their 'promiscuous attendance' with men at dissection or
during clinical exposition. In his opinion such an activity would
imperil their delicacy and purity - the very crown of womanhood -

and react on the courtesy, reverence and tenderness of manhood.

The judicial suggestion that a partition be erected down the middle of the anatomy room similar to the one which segregated male prisoners from female in the Pentonville Prison Chapel, gives a clue to the kind of male-female relationships comprehended in the dominant ideology of the time. What was needed was a screen not between the women's eyes and the nude corpses, but between the women's eyes and the men's eyes. Men might watch women at work on corpses, but these men had to be superiors such as professors supervising students or doctors supervising nurses. Sexual companionship was seen to be inconsistent with work, and work on a basis of equality as incompatible with sexual companionship. The destiny of middle-class women was to be middle-class wives, or, if they failed to marry, middle-class nurses, but it was not to be middle-class doctors. They were to complement men, not compete with them. Where the ethic of individual endeavour conflicted with the concept of the male-dominated family, it was the latter that was to prevail.

Universities claimed to be the centres of reason, doctors the upholders of science and judges the guardians of logic. The combined wisdom of all three should have produced truths of the most formidable degree. Instead it produced academic mythology reinforced by professional mythology reinforced by judicial mythology. The myth of sexual complementarity shrouded the enforced subordination and exclusion of women, the myth of judicial neutrality masked judicial support for male domination, and the myth of professional integrity veiled economic and domestic self-interest.

The medical profession was determined to prevent its ranks from being diluted by the entry of females. In this respect the doctors were no different from any other craft group that had a legal monopoly over payment for the performance of certain types of work. They fought as tenaciously to resist threats to their income and status from a new class of competitors, as skilled artisans did to exclude semi-skilled operatives from certain forms of employment. The exclusion of women from medical practice was thus associated more with professionalism than with prudery. Science and university training were the instruments whereby the doctor was elevated above the empirical healer or midwife. In Britain as in other countries, women had been prominent as healers in the community 'the unlicensed doctors, anatomists and pharmacists of western history' (Ehrenreich and English 1974). Their remedies were dismissed by the male professionals as superstitious lore, to be contrasted with the scientific treatment of qualified practitioners. Women might continue to heal, but only in the ancillary role of nurses under male instruction. The fact was well known that it was primarily women who washed bodies, dressed wounds and attended to the personal needs of injured and diseased patients of both sexes. Furthermore, what passed for science then did as little to cure patients as Victorian prisons did to rehabilitate convicts. In fact, at that time the treatment by leeching and purgatives offered by the male doctors was probably worse than the less drastic ministrations of the female folk-healers.

What is so striking is how illiberal the so-called liberal professions were. The male doctors successfully lobbied Parliament to prevent females from entering their ranks, while male professors and

male lawyers had little difficulty in persuading male judges that
women should be excluded from the campus and the court-room. Yet
this was always done under the claim not of protecting themselves
but of protecting the women. The professional men asserted that
they wished to save female students from going against their nat-
ures, and male students from giving in to theirs. They declared
that they sought to secure the universities against a drop in
standards and the public against incompetent healers, but in fact
they were mainly shielding male purses from female competition.

This, at least, was one of the allegations made by feminists, who
could see no reason in logic or in policy why women of proven ability who wished to become doctors should be debarred from doing so.
Replying to this argument, Lord Deas said in his judgment that it
would be absurd to suggest that the entry of women into medicine was
objected to on grounds of economic jealousy. He declared that opp-
onents of the women conscientiously believed that to let females
into the profession would diminish the delicacy which surrounded
women in well-bred society. It appears, however, that he was well
aware of the spuriousness of this attitude when set against women's
actual role in attending to the ill, but instead of refuting the
myth of female refinement, which would have been distressing to his
male hearers, he reaffirmed it by asserting that when it came to
severe suffering and danger to health, nature itself threw a veil
over delicacy and preserved it uninjured.

The question he did not ask, and could not have been expected to
ask, was why the belief in female delicacy arose and why it was so
fiercely defended in the face of overwhelming contrary evidence. It
is one thing to establish the content of a myth: in this case, that
men were decorous and women possessed of refinement which necessitated that men exempt women from the unpleasant tasks associated with
public and professional life. It is another problem altogether to
determine why the myth existed.

By definition the form of the myth hides rather than reveals the
reason for the myth. A representation must both be manifestly at
variance with everyday observation and sincerely believed in to be a
myth. Its function is precisely to disguise social reality, or
rather, to describe the world in terms favourable to the position of
a particular group. Myth helps to explain what would otherwise be
non-understandable and to justify what would otherwise be non-
acceptable. It transmutes hard conflict into soft poetry, sharp
fact into hazy metaphor, the unpleasant evident into the pallatable
self-evident. If the interest it served could be revealed, it would
dissolve. But myths cannot be disposed of by disputation, since
they essentially relate to belief rather than rationality. Beliefs
structure evidence far more firmly than evidence structures beliefs.
Groups perceive human activities in terms of categories established
by the ideology, using the term ideology again to signify some
systematic world view which describes, explains and justifies a
particular form of social ordering. The rationalisation that is
implicit in ideology need not be logical, it is enough that it be
plausible. Nor need it be expressed systematically or even be consciously entertained. In Britain, where it is the height of political insult to accuse an opponent of being ideological, a person's
ideology is more likely to be an inarticulate conglomerate of

opinions held together by what is termed 'common sense'.

The expression 'male ideology' as used in reference to the judgments in the cases of the women's claims, then, is not intended to
convey that the judges viewed women's position in terms of some
systematic philosophy traceable to the writings of any particular
political philosopher. Nor in suggesting that the judges articulated male ideology is it contended that they were particularly
misogynistic, or in any way conspiratorial; those who wielded power
normally had no need to resort to deviousness, since they could
more easily and safely achieve their purposes by relying on the
values and agencies fashioned to sustain their power. On the
contrary, the more sincere the judges were in their beliefs, the
more effectively could they act upon them.

Male ideology denied the existence of inequity in the treatment
by men of women, and rationalised legal disabilities imposed on
women in terms of each sex having dominion in its separate sphere.
In the context of actual and legal male domination, however, the
theory of complementarity was merely a gracious way of explaining
female subjection. This rationalisation was not something invented
by upper-class Victorian males. There was any amount of literature
on which the judges and others could draw to testify to the subordination of women through the ages. The specific contribution
they made was to place a halo over domesticity, granting to it a
special virtue, and pushing it to an extreme.

The exclusion of women from the professions was directly linked
to domesticity. Middle-class men did not share the objection of
many of the members of the nobility to work, in fact they prided
themselves on their industriousness, nor did they object to women
working, since they employed women to clean and cook in their
homes, as well as to milk and reap on their farms and spin in their
factories. What they did object to, with a vehemence indicative of
a special interest, was to their *own* wives working. Women of the
middle class were first, expected to run households in which the
menfolk could eat, be clothed, entertain and sleep in comfort.
Second, they were to produce sons for business, the professions, the
military and the church, and daughters for good marriages. Third,
they were to display in their households a graciousness, refinement
and sentiment, lacking in the hard world of business, which would
mark off the reputation of their families and maintain the esteem of
their class. It was this third requirement that distinguished the
middle-class woman from her working-class cousin. Working-class
women were also required to look after the home and reproduce sons
and daughters, but they were expected not to attempt graces above
their station. A degree of spending which would indicate taste and
refinement in a middle-class woman, would be castigated as reckless
and profligate if done by a working-class woman. In terms of male
ideology, the model working-class wife was pious and thrifty, qual-
ities which were not inconsistent with work outside the home, while
the prototype middle-class wife, on the other hand, was ornamental
and decorous, attributes which were incompatible with outside
employment.

Superficially it might have seemed that the actions of the legislators in keeping working-class women out of the coal mines were of
a pattern with those designed to exclude middle-class women from the

professions. In both cases the argument was used that women should
be spared unseemly kinds of employment. But even if the language of
justification used in both situations was similar, the interests at
stake were entirely different. The fact that millions of women,
both married and single, worked in paid employment outside the home,
showed that there was no overwhelming biological or cultural aver-
sion to women working for cash. There was nothing intrinsic to the
female condition, no special frailty, that the male legislators and
judges were bent on respecting.

The phrase used at the time was that employment would 'un-sex'
women, to the manifest disadvantage of both sexes. This phrase was
not used in a literal sense, otherwise there would have been difficulty in explaining the notoriously high number of children born of
their masters' to women in domestic service. What was envisaged was
feminity rather than sexuality, that is, female manners rather than
female eroticism. Feminist writers could not contain their indignation at what they considered male hypocrisy in deliberately ignor-
ing the extent to which millions of women were in reality employed
away from their homes, often in laborious and poorly paid jobs. 'In
Staffordshire', wrote one such writer, '(women) make nails; and
unless my readers have seen them, I cannot represent to the imagination the extraordinary figures they represent - black with soot,
muscular, brawny - undelightful to the last degree' (Parkes, 1865,
pp.22-3). Elsewhere, she wrote, there had been a factory strike,
with letters, speeches and placards, and a liberal expenditure of
forcible Saxon language. Who had been these people gathered together
in angry knots on the corners of streets? - Women! It was industry
and not small committees in London, she declared, which should
answer the charge of un-sexing women.

The great battles to exclude women from underground mining and
certain sectors of heavy industry had nothing in common with the
efforts to keep middle-class women out of the professions. The
attacks on female employment in industry were waged largely as
Parliamentary counter-offensives by the landed interests against the
emergent industrialists. The language of humanitarianism was used
to assert the values of rural paternalism against the ethic of
unrestricted industrial enterprise. On the other hand, men of the
gentry and of the industrial class shared an interest in keeping
their wives at home to manage their households, though they were
socially in competition. The extraordinary emphasis on proper
dress, decorum and etiquette for Victorian ladies was tied to
attempts by the industrialists to surpass the gentry not only in
economic and political power, but in manners and self-esteem as well.

It has been said that by the mid nineteenth century the idleness
of the wife was the most sensitive indicator of social standing,
because she became the means whereby the income of the husband was
translated into symbols of respectability. In these terms the
inanity of female existence in prosperous Victorian homes could
become comprehensible if seen as the wife's contribution to the
social esteem of the whole family (Rowbotham, 1973). An ornamental
wife was proof of credit-worthiness both on earth and in heaven,
since only the financially secure could afford the expense of such a
wife, and only those favoured by Providence could be financially
secure. Reputability depended not merely on the display of fortune,

but on the ability to demonstrate sets of manners and codes of conduct superior to those of the country lords and squires. By
cultivating through his wife new refinements even more useless than
those of the country gentleman, the city tradesman was able to claim
social superiority. It was not he who was seen as a ruthless money-
grabber, but the country gentleman who was converted into a silly
bumpkin. As far as the man from the new industrial and commercial
class was concerned, his work routine kept him at home alongside his
wife in the evenings and on week-ends. In contrast to the males of
the landed gentry who devoted considerable spare time to vigorous
physical sports such as riding, shooting, drinking, whoring and
soldiering, he spent his regular hours at home maintaining the
decorum of the household. Whereas the rural gentleman cultivated a
conception of Manhood that emphasised spontaneity, courage and
bearing, the wealthy townsman elevated self-control and spirituality
into the prime virtues of his sex. At the same time, the increasing
manifold and increasingly useless accomplishments of the townsman's
wife were symbols of his increasingly high social status.

Yet the emphasis on the elaborate clothing, cultivated speech and
social refinement of the urban ladies should not be taken as proof
that the role of the middle-class wife was purely ornamental or
symbolical. In addition to being required to display social delicacy, she had to manage what was in effect a large economic and
political enterprise, namely the household. She had to hire and
fire servants, bargain with tradesmen, control children and attend
to the multitudinous needs of her husband. Whether regarded (as by
Mill, Engels and Veblen in their various writings) as a head servant,
or else as a manager, her tasks were detailed and multifarious,
requiring what today would be called great skills in home economics,
personnel management and interpersonal relations. As Mill told
Members of Parliament, women whose chief daily business was the
laying out of money so as to produce the greatest results with the
smallest means, could give lessons to his hearers who contrived to
produce such singularly poor results with such vast means.

The vaunted complementarity of the sexes, invariable expressed in
semi-mystical terms, had practical roots in a division of labour in
respect of which the husband supervised minions at work and the wife
supervised minions at home. Different attributes were required for
the performance of their respective tasks, and these attributes were
given exaggerated reflection in the culture of the times. It is
suggested, then, that the main reason why Victorian men resisted the
entry of middle-class women into public life and the professions,
was their interest in ensuring that their wives remained house-
keepers. Mill certainly hinted at such, adding that it was a reason
which men were ashamed to advance because of its manifest injustice.

If correct, this hypothesis helps to explain two otherwise puzz-
ling phenomena. The first is that the middle-class sections of the
suffragette movement aroused far greater antagonism from middle-
class men than did the working-class section. One might have
anticipated that middle-class men would have assented more readily
to the vote being granted to their mothers, wives, sisters and
daughters, who were likely to share their values and allegiances,
than to working-class womenfolk who were socially and politically
distant from them. Yet the enfranchisement of propertyless working

women appears to have been looked on with greater equanimity than the enfranchisement of propertied ladies. This is evidenced by the fact that when Prime Minister Asquith chose, in what is generally regarded as the turning point in the campaign for votes for women, to receive a deputation of suffragette women, he selected working-class women from the East London Federation headed by Sylvia Pankhurst rather than women from the large middle-class suffrage groups. The second apparent paradox clarified by this hypothesis, is that middle-class women increasingly entered the professions at a time when the number of domestic servants was declining. It seems that possession of servants, far from freeing middle-class women from domesticity, tied them to their homes. Supervising servants became a career in itself which acted to exclude all other careers. Middle-class men accordingly shared an interest in keeping their wives at home and away from professional work and in preparing their daughters for similar domestic vocations.

A century after the courts had decided that it was unlawful in England to use force to keep a slave in the house, lawyers were still maintaining that it was permissible to use force to keep a wife in the house. An Englishman's home was his castle, and her prison. When in the celebrated Clitheroe case the judges finally held that a writ of 'habeas corpus' should issue against a husband who with his solicitor's aid had kidnapped and confined his runaway wife (Queen v. Jackson, 1891, Q.B.D. 671) the court was condemned by 'The Times' for weakening the institution of marriage. What this case reveals, however, is that the judiciary and legislature were slowly modernising and rationalising aspects of the middle-class marriage and bringing family law into line with the new kinds of family home and family property that were developing.

The task of the feminist campaigners was facilitated by profound changes that were taking place in the character of the family and the nature of property. In formal terms, the family remained the same, its legal basis continuing to be the Christian monogamous marriage. Similarly, the major legal classifications of property were still based on distinctions between land and things separate from land. However, industrialisation under conditions of capital-ism transformed the social situation of the family and created entirely new forms of wealth. As O.R. McGregor (5) has put it, the nineteenth century saw a transformation of entrepreneurial activity brought about by the creation of a national capital market through the Stock Exchange and a national labour market through the Poor Laws. Parliament also recognised limited liability companies as an incentive for the investment of capital, and set up the Board of Trade to regulate companies; it was state intervention, therefore, that provided the basis for laissez faire. He might have gone further and suggested that these processes also paved the way for reforming the law relating to the family.

As soon as land ceased to be the main form of property and chief index of wealth and status, new forms of family law and rules of inheritance could be developed. In the eighteenth century the device of the trust settlement was used to protect a daughter's inheritance from being squandered by a profligate husband. In the nineteenth century, after much campaigning by feminist groups, married women were authorised by statute to hold property separately

from their husbands. The Married Women's Property Act 1882 is often
held out as a milestone in the march of women to equality, but in
reality it did little more than save wealthy women from the irksome
restraints of holding property through trustees. In fact men continued to control the property of women, even if only in the capacity
of advisers rather than as husbands or trustees, since women were
precluded from acquiring the skills thought to be needed for the
proper administration of their property, such skills being securely
located within the male professions. Since few married women were
able to earn sufficient to acquire their own property, the effects
of the Act were necessarily limited, and although the man who
drafted the basis of the Act, Dr Richard Pankhurst, supported sexual
equality in every sphere, the Members of Parliament who let the
measure go through unopposed, did so generally because they saw it
as an alternative to granting women greater public rights. The law
went some way towards protecting wives from being abused inside the
home; it did not create opportunities for them to be useful outside
the home. A curb on spending by husbands was not the same as a
licence to earn independently by wives. Thus the destiny of woman
as wife rather than independent person was enhanced rather than
reduced by the Act.

Feudal law had merged the legal person of the wife with that of
the husband, a legal arrangement appropriate to land-based wealth,
where the family lands, house and name remained intact from generation to generation through eldest sons. It was the growth of
limited liability companies in the nineteenth century that created
new forms of economic power divorced from ownership of land, and
that relegated the home from the public domain to the domestic
sphere. This was the converse of the process noted by Karl Renner
(6), in terms of which property increasingly lost its private and
family character and became public in function; he gave the example
of the railway station and the laundry which were still described by
law as privately owned but which in social practice had become
public utilities. These two simultaneous developments - the home
becoming private and the land becoming public - were not inconsistent. Increasingly the home was being separated from the land on
which it stood and from productive activity. The factory system
destroyed family industry, and the home lost its character as the
centre of work and became instead a place of rest and reproduction.
The home was domesticated, as was the role of women in it. Women's
work in the home became an end in itself, extolled for its own sake
and incorporated by men into the myth of femininity.

The domestication of the home drastically reduced women's public
influence, and converted relatively independent wives, whose
contribution to production had given them a strong position within
the family, into totally dependent housewives. Yet despite the
near-complete public subordination of the middle-class housewife,
the judges extolled the position of the Englishwoman as being
without compare. Judge Willes declared the honour and respect in
which women were held to be one of the glories of British civilisation. Similarly, Lord Ardmillan stressed that, because the elevation
of women in domestic and social position was one of the blessed
fruits of Christianity, it was especially necessary to keep women
out of mixed anatomy classes.

Experience in the Empire, however, suggested a different variant
on the theme of the relationship between Christianity, women and
work, and possibly helps explain why British women were alleged to
be in so favoured a position. In many colonies the major objective
of British policy was said to be to teach the indigenous inhabitants
the dignity of labour. By this was meant labour in the employ of
British settlers or administrators, since no amount of labour by
indigenous inhabitants on their own land was regarded as dignified.
The destruction of the self-sufficient traditional family was a pre-
requisite for employment, and it was to further this end that the
menfolk of Britain, so reluctant to grant rights to their own wives,
became so solicitous about the rights of women in colonised societies. In his work on the legal status of African women, Jack
Simons (1968) remarks that colonists in southern Africa complained
that the tribesman had too much land, leisure and sex. Instead of
earning his living by the sweat of his brow in proper employment,
the tribesman allegedly battened in ease on the labour of his wife.
African women were said by colonists to be hardly better off than
slaves, and polygyny was described as being less a form of marriage
than a licensed system of lust, which enabled a privileged class of
cattle-owners to live in sensual indolence at the expense of their
womenfolk. Simons points out that this colonialist sexual myth had
little substance. In reality the tribesmen had attained a high
standard of political and legal organisation, they observed a strict
moral code, and governed themselves with dignity and self-restraint.
'The pity showered on the women', he writes, 'was largely misplaced.
They did not constitute a separate class, were not oppressed, and
were not segregated behind a tribal kind of purdah. They shared the
rank of their fathers and husbands, and held an honoured, if junior
position in their domestic households.' Nevertheless, he observes,
the banner of Christianity, progress and female emancipation provided a moral pretext for invading African territory and forcing
peasants on to the land.

Irony is intrinsic to myth, and so it is not all that surprising
that the colonial sexual myth was later turned around to reinforce
the metropolitan sexual myth. Lord Curzon, one of the leaders of
the anti-suffrage movement, declared from his experience as a former
Viceroy of India that the hundreds of millions of subjects in the
Empire could never continue to have respect for the Imperial Government if they got to know that it had been put into office by the
votes of women.

Nor was Lord Ardmillan correct in his assertion that the social
position of women had been elevated by Christianity, certainly not
in its English reformed version. In fact, changes in the institutions of Christianity in Britain contributed substantially to a
decline in the status of women in public life. The digests of
arguments addressed by counsel on behalf of the women in the nineteenth century male-monopoly cases, indicate that prior to the
English Reformation, women's religious orders had played a prominent
role in church and hence public life, and that abbesses and
prioresses had had a respected place in councils of government. In
the period before the end of the sixteenth century, women had voted
in Parliamentary elections, acted as attorneys, held leading
positions in trading guilds, and even occupied high military office.

It would seem that although in feudal times the law of succession
had favoured elder sons, it had not excluded women from inheriting
titles to land and to family position in the absence of a male heir.
Thus the public position of women had been stronger in the sixteenth century than it was at the time when the judges were speaking.

Three factors seem to have contributed to the decline of women's
status over the centuries, the first being the destruction of the
nunneries, associated with the extension of Royal power and the
financing of the army and navy. As one sardonic writer put it, the
exclusion of abbesses from Parliament completed a process of
political inequality begun with the expulsion of Eve from Paradise.
It is notable that even today, the position of women in the Church
in Britain continues to be weaker than it was five hundred years
ago; only the armed forces (another body of men distinguished by
their livery) can equal the ministry for the rigidity with which
they exclude women. A second reason for the decline in women's
public position was the growth of Parliament and the replacement of
hereditary office by appointed office. In this sense, the development of Parliament was profoundly undemocratic in that at the very
time when it denounced the principle of hereditary supremacy it
entrenched the principle of sexual supremacy. The only hereditary
public office which survived was that of the monarchy. It is more
than a little paradoxial that during the period under review it was
possible for a woman to hold the highest office in the land but not
the lowest. It was Queen Victoria who summoned the legislators and
in whose name the judges acted, yet both Parliament and the judiciary
refused to acknowledge a general right of women to hold public
office. Presumably from the sixteenth century onwards it was
regarded as preferable to have a Protestant woman from a British
family on the throne than a Catholic man from a French or Spanish
one. A third factor which diminished women's position in public
life was the growth of the professions and the establishment of the
universities.

The separation of knowledge from production and of work from the
home, drastically weakened the economic and political situation of
women. In the medieval artisan and trading guilds, women were
normally subordinate to their fathers and husbands, but not necessarily to their sons. Widows frequently took over control of the
family tools and the running of the family enterprise, and exercised
correlative influence in the guilds. The universities were residential in character, and accordingly from the first favoured men,
who could more easily live away from home than women. Britain in
fact appears to be unique amongst industrialised societies in the
extent to which single-sex education has persisted, and the males-
only principle is most strongly maintained in the oldest schools
and colleges, which either exclude females altogether or else admit
only a tiny quota. Oxford and Cambridge were in fact the last
rather than the first universities to admit women to degrees,
Cambridge resisting until 1948. Universities claim to be the
inheritors of truth and the upholders of merit, yet as far as women
were concerned, they were manifestly citadels of intolerance.
Similarly, the professions controlled entry into their ranks by
requiring extensive training either at university or in the form of
apprenticeship away from home. A widow could not inherit a husband's

legal or medical practice, because law and medicine were early converted into professions requiring knowledge of Latin and philosophy,
neither of which were particularly helpful in healing or in
resolving disputes, but both of which were of great assistance in
displaying the special sort of learning that entitled its possessor
to a special fee.

Whereas the medical profession expressly set out to take healing
away from women - many female folk-healers being condemned on the
testimony of professional male doctors as witches - the legal
profession established a monopoly of litigation and conveyancing
which only incidentally excluded females. The procedures designed
to protect the income and status of the professional lawyers from
the competition of unregistered scribes and other unqualified
persons were not specifically anti-feminist, but their consequences
were to make it impossible for women to practise law. Once this
exclusion of females had been established, however, male-ness
became part of the ethos of the profession, and male-exclusiveness
was elevated to the level of a principle. A legal profession
centralised around the courts in London as opposed to community
lawyers dispersed through the population, favoured the exclusion of
women. In the neighbourhoods there were of course wise women as
well as wise men who were consulted and asked to arbitrate inform-
ally on local disputes, but since they did not work for a fee in
association with the courts, they were not regarded as lawyers.

The above analysis is offered as at least part explanation of why
upper-middle-class men who prided themselves on their loftiness of
purpose and rationality of method, should have behaved with such
social brutality towards women of their own class. The contention
is that underlying the behaviour of men such as the judges was a
twofold material interest structured around gender: first, that
women should continue to serve men in the domestic sphere at home,
and second, that they should not swell the ranks of competitors at
work. To some extent middle-class women have been freed from their
function as 'head-servants' by the destruction of the servant-based
middle-class household, but otherwise the two material considerations
are as operative today as they were a century ago. This suggests
that male intransigence is not simply a cultural relic which is
fated to vanish with outmoded patriarchy, but rather that it is the
expression of persisting self-interest which may be expected to
spawn ever-new rationalisations. At the same time, however, the
legal and political gains made by women in earlier generations of
struggle, together with those established more recently, puts them
in a stronger position to tackle the continuing inequality, and to
carry along with them the growing body of men willing to be dis-
lodged from their positions of dominance.

NOTES

1 This case concerned the right of women to be nominated for the
   Canadian Senate in 1929.
2 These cases are dealt with more fully in 'Sexism and the Law',
   Albie Sachs and Joan Hoff Wilson, Martin Robertson, 1977.
3 Karslake, Essex, House of Commons Debates, 20 May 1867.

4   Deacon and Hill (1972), p.94, reference to Harriet Martineau in the 'Edinburgh Review', April 1859.
5   O.R. McGregor, unpublished lecture delivered at Bedford College, Summer 1973.
6   See extracts from Karl Renner in V. Aubert (1972).

3 Doctors and their patients
The social control of women in general practice

Michèle Barrett and Helen Roberts

Other articles in this volume explore the ways in which women and
female sexuality are subjected to social control. It is now well
known that in matters such as contraception and abortion the medical
profession has exercised a degree of power over women which is
disproportionate to the importance of the technical expertise upon
which this influence and control is supposedly based. There are,
however, more subtle ways in which the medical profession acts as an
institution of control, and in the examination of the relationship
between the middle-aged woman and her doctor the social as opposed
to the medical aspects of this control become apparent.

Doctors are educated to see their patients as examples of individual pathology rather than as products of pathology in the social
structure. Consequently when a patient presents with a particular
complaint at the surgery, the general practitioner will tend to
assume that the complaint either has a physical basis (which can be
diagnosed and treated), or that it is of a 'psychosomatic' character.
This latter concept has in recent years been widely accepted through-
out the medical profession as well as by the general public. As
well as the term's neutral meaning of a physical illness with a
hypothesised mental origin, the label 'psychosomatic' frequently
carries the connotation of the patient's supposed failure to with-
stand the strains of everyday life in modern society.

As far as men are concerned, there tends to be considerable
understanding of and sympathy for the pressures experienced by the
ambitious middle-class man in a competitive economy. GPs themselves
are commonly middle-class men working under some pressure, and will
identify with problems of overwork and heavy responsibility,
although they may still retain the notion of personal failure as
appropriate to the man who actually breaks down under such pressure.
In the case of middle-aged women the GP is less likely to identify
with the frustration and anxiety presented to him and more likely
to ascribe the symptoms to individual inadequacy rather than to a
structurally determined lack of opportunity. In the woman's case,
of course, her failure is located in the family rather than in any
life she may lead outside the home. Hence her problems are seen by
GPs to be those of marital difficulty, of facing up to the menopause
and the emptying of the nest, and of the need to find some small

interest outside the home to while away her time.

In our research (1) on the consulting patterns of middle-aged women we found recurring instances of the GP attributing a supposedly psychosomatic complaint to the acknowledged boredom of his patient's life. This knowledge, however, did not lead either the GP or the patient to question the framework of her life or to challenge its determination by her past or present family obligations. In consult-ation after consultation the GP smooths away the surface anxiety and adjusts the woman to the limitations of a life located totally in a home from which the children have moved away. In this respect the institution of medicine legitimates and endorses the status quo in relation to the position of women, and in so doing it fulfils an ideological function as a agency of disguised social control. We found that frequently doctors would use the authority of their medico-moral language to offer not neutral, clinical, advice but a set of prescriptions based on the conventional wisdom of their own social milieu.

In this paper we should like to document some recent data bearing on the points made above. We shall describe ways in which not only general practitioners but also hospital specialists (particularly in the psychiatric field) relate to women in terms of non-medical, social criteria. We shall also give examples of the attitudes towards their doctors held by women in this age group, and the extent to which they accept the authority and control of the medical pro-fession over their lives. These examples are taken from interviews with women who were known to consult their GP very rarely as well as women who consult very frequently. In conclusion we shall try to summarise the evidence supporting the assertion that the GP may act as an agent of social control, looking particularly at the profes-sion's rear-guard action against the new ideas about health and self-help put forward by the Women's Movement.

Before going into some of the very conservative attitudes found among doctors in relation to women and the family, we should perhaps indicate briefly some important characteristics of the medical profession. Sociologists of medicine have in the past accepted too readily a medically oriented, epidemiological account of their subject-matter and have not sufficiently queried the social charac-teristics of the practitioners of medicine. As a profession, medicine has high prestige and tends to recruit from a middle-class population, and we should not let the pastoral image of the practice of medicine blind us to the real power wielded by the institution.

Goffman's (1961) description of the control exercised by the psychiatric hospital has now found echoes in the analysis of general medicine. Irving Zola (1975) has argued that not only does medicine operate as an institution of control, but that it has successfully expanded its empire in recent years. Zola points out that doctors are now applied to for advice on environmental, technical, religious or psychiatric matters which are frequently beyond the scope of a medical education. Since medical advice carries the force of a moral imperative this practice is a particularly bad one, as Robinson has pointed out when he referred to 'the insidious and largely undramatic process of making medicine and the labels "healthy" and "ill" relevant to an ever increasing part of human existence' (1973, p.107).

Modern medical practice can be seen to reflect not only the power of a traditional elite grouping within the bourgeoisie but also that of drug-manufacturing companies and the developing private sector. The scale of profits from the pharmaceutical industry has recently become widely known (Klass, 1975), and it is not a coincidence that one of the largest groups of patients taking psychotropic drugs is that of middle-aged women.

The obvious profitability (in terms of time for the doctor) of adjustment via pills must have contributed to the medical profession's unwillingness to discuss the real problems confronted by middle-aged women. Without entering here into a lengthy treatment of the economics of medical prescribing patterns, it is worth noting that medical advertising for profitable tranquillizers systematically presents the housewife as the patient and beneficiary of the drug (Stimson, 1975). Medicine is not only an institution of social control, it is a particularly male-dominated one.

This male dominance is reflected in the sociology of medicine, which has not so far systematically challenged the sexist practices of its subject. The classic sociological study of medical education encapsulates the problem in its title - 'Boys in White' (Becker et al., 1961). Sociologists have failed to comment on the low proportion of women in the profession, on the fact that women are virtually absent from high positions in medicine, and that although women form a numerical majority of general health workers, they are concentrated in low-status positions. The profession itself has not systematically confronted this problem, although evidence now exists which demonstrates the irrational basis of the discrimination. Bewley and Bewley (1975), leaving aside the question of whether the woman doctor *should* be more responsible for her family than the man doctor, have indicated that the rate at which women doctors leave the profession through family obligations is not significantly higher than the rate for men doctors attributable to alcoholism, emigration, involuntary removal from the Medical Register, and so on.

Since neither sociologists nor the medical profession have faced the issue of male dominance, it has been left to feminists to document the extent to which sexism abounds in this profession. Scully and Bart's (1973) classic analysis of gynaecological text books demonstrated attitudes towards female sexuality which were unenlightened by even the widely disseminated findings of the post-war American sexology surveys. A succession of subsequent papers have documented several further aspects of conservatism in the profession. It is not however sufficient to simply state that the medical profession shares interests with other bourgeois patriarchal institutions, and in the following we hope to describe some of the specific mechanisms which operate in general practice.

In our research we have studied the average local GP (usually a middle-aged man), rather than sought out the rarer progressive, experimental doctor. Conversations with GPs who espouse left-wing or self-help or feminist views merely serve to confirm the numerical insignificance and powerlessness of such persons in the profession as a whole. Although our sample is a small one, there seems no reason to believe that it is not representative of the profession.(2)

Working with GPs over some time it became clear to us that our respondents made certain unspoken assumptions about the 'nature' of men and women. Men, it was clear, had a primary, natural 'drive' to work to support their wife and family. Women had a similar 'drive' to nourish and cherish their husband and family. These assumptions, so fundamental to the ideological structure of patriarchal capitalism (and evident constantly in the media, religion, political discourse and so on), are not merely reflected in the practice of medicine but are actively endorsed and sanctioned with medical authority. Numerous cases were found, for example, of a woman performing two jobs (one inside the home and one in paid employment) and suffering from symptoms of stress, anxiety and tiredness. Occasionally a doctor might in such circumstances suggest cautiously that some of the housework could be shared among the family, but this would be rare. The common response was to advise the woman to give up her job. Not only might this advice come from the GP, we also found it advocated by the psychiatrists to whom the women had been referred. Many of the women patients we interviewed had been given, and followed, such advice.

We are not wishing to deny the existence of cases where medical conditions preclude a woman working outside the home, but merely wish to show how much doctors differentiate between women and men in this respect. In fact, doctors tend to see their male patients almost exclusively in terms of their occupation. Our GP respondents said to us that the average middle-aged man (not consulting for concrete organic illness) would be consulting for worries about jobs, about money, about too much responsibility at work, or the threat of redundancy. One doctor described the effects of entering middle age for men solely in terms of the implications for his work - that men in manual jobs found their health deteriorating, their blood pressure rising, and that men in executive positions found their mental capacities impaired and their responsibilities over-whelming. Not only did he not see family circumstances as relevant to the man's health, he maintained that this was a 'natural' phenomenon. Women, he argued, were 'naturally' bound to their children and men to their jobs. If marital problems arose, they were problems for the woman rather than the man, since by definition she was more dependent upon the marriage than he was.

Another GP took yet further the 'natural' basis of the male's identification with his job, and actually claimed that any man not positively motivated to work to support his family must be in need of psychiatric care. Thus he rejected the notion that a man might 'malinger' (in order to obtain a certificate for sick leave) since he thought that any man feigning illness must be psychologically unbalanced. There could be no rational desire for a man to evade work.

The importance of work to the man is paralleled in the woman's case by family obligations, and the GPs in our sample showed no spontaneous awareness of any kind of role conflict experienced by women with obligations both at home and at work. They perceived 'working women' as ordinary housewives and mothers who had a tiring time as a result of their laudable and necessary efforts to supplement the family income. No conflict was perceived between a desire to maintain the family and to lead an individual life outside the

home, although many of the women we interviewed said that they were
employed for interest and company rather than for additional housekeeping money.

Our sample of doctors (largely suburban and not much concerned
with what they termed 'career women') felt that work for a woman was
either a financial necessity, as with the working-class mother with
young children, or a convenient way of passing time when the children
had left home. One doctor said that he would often advise a middle-
aged woman with no children at home to take a part-time job. He
indicated that a short shift in a local factory was ideal for such
women (i.e., low pay, unskilled work, no job security, no promotion
and so on). In denying the importance of paid work for women, these
doctors were then free to stress that the husband, home and family
were the woman's prime responsibility. They acknowledged that this
was a burden of which the housewife could never be free, that even
if she was herself too ill to cope she would make every effort to do
so and would not rest properly. One phrased this in terms of the
husband's laziness and reluctance to help in the house, another in
terms of the wives' strong motivation to be loyal to their families
and care for them above all else. Whichever way you phrase it, the
primary obligation is clear.

It is interesting to note that at the same time as locating men
in terms of their occupations and women in terms of their families,
our doctors repeatedly commented that women had vague and spurious
worries. Men, they claimed, had particular physical or occupational
problems which brought them to the surgery, whereas women seemed to
'worry about nothing'. This was said particularly frequently in
relation to patients whom GPs described as 'psychosomatic'. They
perceived middle-aged women as exhibiting more psychosomatic complaints than men. However, perception of a middle-aged woman as a
'psychosomatic' patient did nothing to ensure sympathetic treatment.
Some doctors were decidedly unsympathetic, even though they might
have some insight into the social background of the woman's problems,
and other doctors responded well only to patients with whom they had
an obvious personal rapport. In no case did a GP comment that a
person's having, as they described it, 'nothing to worry about' was
in itself a disadvantage. They did not seem aware that for these
women the determining problem was an enforced lack of meaning,
independence and identity. They appreciated only that the middle-
aged woman who had no interests outside the home would be bored, and
they appreciated that the menopause might bring depression related
to feelings of uselessness.

In describing these attitudes and assumptions held by GPs we hope
to show how they inform and determine the treatment given to middle-
aged women. In trying to establish patterns of treatment we
followed certain cases through to any consultants to which they had
been referred. GPs of course vary in the degree to which they
would refer a person to a specialist, and perhaps particularly so in
the case of a woman they suspect to be a 'psychosomatic' patient.
However, it was in pursuing the hospital and private consultants,
and especially those in the psychiatric service, that we found the
strongest evidence of control.

A GP confronted by a frustrated woman (either tied to a young
family or bored because she is bereft of her children) does not

confront a strictly medical problem. He faces the product of a social system which forces a woman to choose between a job and an interest in life outside the family, and a life bound up in the home. For many women this is not, or certainly was not, a real choice, and so the plight of the housebound mother or frustrated older woman is not the result of a rationally planned course of action but the inevitable consequence of not defying the strongest of conventions. The GP, then, is confronted by a person whose condition has been determined by the social system rather than by exclusively individual problems or inadequacies. This recognition tends to be precluded by a traditional medical education, since the training concentrates largely on personal pathology.(3) Hence, we argue, the GP has virtually no choice but to see the woman in question either in terms of the conventional models of his own social background (she must learn to adjust to her situation), or in terms of individual personal inadequacy (that she must be referred to a psychiatrist).

In our cases we found the GP was often prepared to refer a woman to a psychiatrist if he found himself beaten or 'floored' by her problems. For example one doctor described a woman who presented with a series of illnesses which he said were 'hysterical' or psycho-somatic. He could not understand why this should be the case, since the woman had 'a doting husband, a nice home and lovely kids.' It certainly did not occur to him that however excellent her domestic circumstances might be, she might lack other sources of meaning to her life. Certainly we found no instances of a GP challenging the assumption that a married woman's life was exclusively oriented towards her family, and the most usual policy would be sympathy, adjustment, drugs, and in the end if all else failed, referral to a psychiatrist. It seems possible that if closer links existed between GPs and the social work system and if the latter had exten-sive counselling facilities for women then GPs would refer many women to them instead of to a psychiatrist. Although the social work system may likewise operate as an agency of social control, it does not define the individual so acutely as a sick person. As it is many anxious and frustrated women are sent in desperation to the psychiatrist as the GP sees no one else more suitable available, and this referral itself reinforces the woman's sense of individual failure.

We found examples of the psychiatric system being used in the manipulative ways described by Goffman (1961), Laing (1965) and others. Women were quite remorselessly confirmed in traditional family and domestic roles and more than one instance of a woman's refusal to do housework resulted eventually in hospitalisation and ECT. As mentioned earlier, the psychiatrists in question would normally advise that the woman give up her paid work rather than attempt to reorganise the division of labour at home. It is perhaps symptomatic of the status hierarchy in medicine that the psychia-trists with whom we had contact were more blatantly superior and patronising than the GPs in the way they referred to their middle-aged female patients. Invariably such women were 'settled neurotics' or 'drips' or 'hypochondriacs' and invariably also their husbands or consorts were 'sensible' 'long-suffering' men.

Other ways in which women were offensively patronised included

the common practice of referring to women in their 40s and 50s as
girls ('this poor girl'), or of referring to them in terms of their
social status as derived from their husband ('wife of a golfing
friend of mine'). We also noted that a doctor could sometimes be
influenced by attitudes of the husband of the woman concerned,
despite the possibility that these attitudes had themselves contributed to the woman's difficulties. It was not uncommon for a GP
to identify himself with the long-suffering husband of a neurotic
woman, and indeed one or two of our medical respondents explicitly
drew a parallel between their own wives and this type of patient.
This process is illustrated by the case of one woman who was
referred to a psychiatrist on the advice of a consultant physician
dealing with an injury she had received earlier. This particular
woman wanted to return to full-time employment now that her children
were grown up, but complained that she did not feel physically well
enough to cope with the entire responsibility of the house and
family. Her husband suggested to the physician that she was well
enough to do the housework, and that her demands for help with this
in order for her to go out to work were causing deterioration in
family relations. The consultant physician recorded that this
information from the husband 'confirmed my view that a psychiatric
opinion may be of value'.

It is important to note these attitudes, as GPs and specialists
are in a position of authority over their patients. This power is
particularly strong in the case of anxious middle-aged women who
tend to collude with a definition of themselves as less important
and less useful than their husbands or children. In order to
examine the relationship between doctor and patient we have to look
carefully at the ways in which the woman herself perceives the GP.
In our study we were particularly interested in women who saw the
doctor very frequently, and especially if this high consultation
rate had no obvious physical basis. It is often these women to
whom the GP may be sympathetic or reassuring (or may be patronising);
but it is also these women who at the same time are constantly
encouraged to adjust to rather than challenge the situation of their
lives.

Perhaps we should clarify here that one would not expect a
relatively conservative institution such as the medical profession
to offer its clients a radical critique of their social situation,
and in this paper we are not suggesting that the profession is
failing in its own terms of reference. Nevertheless, such institutions, by their sanctioning of the status quo and their readiness to
blame the individual rather than the society, do exercise considerable resistance to changes which would benefit many who are less
privileged than members of the medical profession.(4) This is, of
course, our own point of view, and was certainly not shared by the
women patients of this age group in our sample.

We referred above to a possible collusion between patient and
doctor in the maintenance of the power relationship between the two.
One does not have to go far to seek the reasons for this, particularly in terms of serious physical illness. Reassurance from, and
confidence in the expertise of one's physician are clearly not only
comforting, but no doubt also instrumental in treatment. What is
interesting is the extent to which the deference and dependency

necessary from the patient to maintain the power relationship are
present not only in high consulters, but also in those who do not
visit the general practitioner frequently.

Attitudes found among both high and low consulters in our sample
were a reluctance to criticise, sometimes in the face of off-hand
not to say negligent treatment, and a strong awareness of their
doctor's heavy workload. This awareness is no doubt empirically
justified. Certainly the doctors in our sample were extremely hard
working and conscientious, but it is noticeable that there is a much
greater willingness to allow for a doctor's heavy work load, than
to make allowances for the heavy work load of those in professions
such as social work - or indeed other walks of life such as the work
load of a supermarket cashier or a dustman. A typical low consulter
commented:
    'I mean, I always think the doctor's a busy person and I mean,
    years ago, when you had to pay for the doctor, you got over your
    ailments unless it was something really serious.'
While another, talking in the same vein said:
    'I wouldn't rush to the doctor's. I never have. I've got this
    thing you know. The doctors, they have such a terribly busy
    life.'
There seemed to be some ambivalence however, particularly among the
high consulters, about whether it was fairer to go to the doctor or
fairer to stay away. One high consulter remarked:
    'I doctor myself, as far as, you know, if it's a cold ... I hang
    on and hang on. Mind you, it's wrong, because you're not fair to
    the doctor.'
While another frequent attender, conveniently living next door to
the surgery endorsed the view that it is 'fairer' to consult the
doctor as soon as possible:
    'If I feel rough I think, oh I'll call in on Dr X. I don't
    believe in playing around. If I have something which I think
    after a day or two I ought to see him about - I just go. I
    think it's no good messing about. You get cured much quicker
    don't you.'
So that while on the one hand, one 'ought' not to bother the doctor
with minor complaints as he is so busy, one 'ought' to be fair to
him by consulting before the disease has had time to get a grip.

The nearest that any of our respondents got to a recognition of
the power relationship between themselves and the doctor was in
describing their fear on going to the surgery. This was not a fear
of what might be wrong with them, but a fear of what the doctor
might think if there was not anything seriously wrong:
    'I sit in that waiting room and keep rehearsing what I have to
    say. Well, he is a busy man - he's a marvellous bloke. ... I
    get too scared I think that's the trouble with a lot of women
    you know. A lot I've spoken to, my friends.'
The same woman admitted:
    'I'm terrible. I send my husband. He goes for me. I get so
    scared and het up .... Once I'm reassured I don't worry',
thus combining her fear and her need for reassurance. As mentioned
above, several women in our sample had been told by their doctors
that they ought not to work outside the home, for reasons of either
physical or mental health. Notwithstanding this, more than one of

these women had taken on extra responsibilities in the form of foster
or adopted children as an alternative to paid employment. There
does not seem to have been any suggestion from the doctor that
unpaid domestic labour of this type might be just as taxing as paid
employment. One woman who had spent a good deal of time in hospital
with debilitating migraine, and subsequently fostered a mongol child
commented:

'I've got more time on my hands than what I've ever had ....
I've taken on this little girl and she comes week-ends. Week-
ends and holidays. I've always wanted to foster, always, and
with Dr Y saying I shouldn't work, it was too much for me, ...
it was best, you know, not to work ....'

Because the 'rights' which one has within the health service are
limited, and one must ask rather than demand, any help given is
frequently seen as a personal favour given by the doctor or the
hospital authority. One of our respondents, herself a very low
consulter, who said: 'I think it's perhaps wrong to go to the
doctors. They're too busy' looked after her bedridden mother for
ten years. It was only when she was on the point of collapse that
she asked the GP if her mother could go into hospital for a few
weeks so that she could have a rest: 'Dr Y. He was very good. He
got her into hospital to give me this break.' The hospital was
not so good however:

'We'd never asked for any help before. We never asked for
anything. We asked if she could stay .... He was very kind,
but he upset my husband terribly because he said - he was a very
nice man, I've nothing against him at all - but he turned to my
husband and said ...'

Even when there are criticisms then, such is the deference of the
average patient towards the medical profession that these will be
couched in the mildest of terms and with a good deal of understanding for the problems of the doctor. Indeed our patient
respondents were a good deal more understanding of their doctors,
than the doctors of their patients. Not for our respondents the
radical critique of the medical profession.

If for our high consulters, the social control of the doctor can
be seen through excessive deference, dependence and need for reassurance, what of the low consulters? Do they visit the doctor in-
frequently as a result of lack of confidence in him, or an unwillingness to trust themselves to conventional medicine? As far as our
respondents are concerned, this was not the case. Without
exception, they saw their good health in terms of luck (and indeed,
all 'touched wood' when referring to it). We felt that this was
symptomatic of a situation where patients feel that they have no
control over or knowledge of their own bodies. If they go wrong,
it is bad luck, if they go right, it is good luck:

'Touch wood ... I think in all my life since I got married, I had
one day when I went to bed and I couldn't get up cause every time
I stood up, I was sick. So that lasted about one day and my
eldest daughter was about 11 or 12 and she coped. The only time
I've ever been in bed was when I had the kiddies. Touch wood.'

In so far as our low consulters did suffer ill health, it was
usually because of their wish not to 'bother' the doctor that they
did not consult. As one said:

'Sometimes you gets a bit depressed, but then you looks around
the world, you sees what goes on and you thinks, what you got to
moan about, you know. I never had to bother the doctor....'
There was one point on which high consulters, low consulters and
doctors all agreed and this was that he was there to 'help' them.
Neither group saw medical treatment as a right, paid for by social
security and taxation. Both saw it in terms of help from an individual for which intense gratitude was due. One grateful patient
remarked:

'E's the best, old Dr Z. Because if you call 'im, 'e's there.
And you can go down and see 'im .... I mean he's got the patience
of a saint ... and 'e never gets irritated. How 'e finds time I
dunno because 'e's always busy.'

It might be suggested that it is this very intense personal relationship between doctor and patient which helps in maintaining the
doctor's control. Patients are not encouraged to see their doctor
as a technician with a certain expertise as they might a car
mechanic. He is very much more.

As we have shown above, middle-aged women tend to perceive the
GP in deferential terms, being grateful to him for his help and
support and yet aware of the demands they make on his already
burdened time. This leads to a classic dependency syndrome, which
makes the dependent woman unlikely to perceive the true nature of
the relationship between herself and the doctor. We found that
time after time the woman patient in this situation would present
herself as anxious, suppliant, dependent, inadequate and unable to
understand the source of her worries and ill health. The doctor and
patient would then collude to produce a consultation in which the
real problems were left undiscussed and the woman was simply confirmed in her identity as wife and mother. In this we maintain that
the traditional attitudes conveyed with supposedly neutral medical
authority constitute a form of social control. This can be made
clearer by considering the consequences that might follow the
absence of a source of paternalistic, sympathetic support from the
doctor.

If such support was not available to women, presumably the
isolation of their position and the difficulties with which many
are burdened would lead to a mugh higher rate of collapse and
breakdown. Many of our women respondents claimed that they
wouldn't be able to cope without the doctor's help. Such breakdown
would among other things act as a severe strain on the functioning
of the family and would contribute to the problems of an institution
which is central to the maintenance of our economic system. More
constructively, it may be argued that if women were denied this
support and help with 'adjustment' from the medical profession, they
might well derive it from other women in a similar situation. It is
the very isolation of the housewife that renders her least likely to
challenge and change her situation and any increase in female
solidarity can readily be seen as a threat to a patriarchal society.
The solidaristic power of the Women's Movement to date has demonstrated this threat very clearly, in a way that is particularly
relevant to the theme of this paper. Not only does the Women's
Movement offer solidarity and a means of ending the isolation
experienced by many women, it has also offered a political perspective

on women's health and the control of women's fertility. The rise of
the women's self-help health movement can be seen as a direct
reaction to the medical tradition of rendering knowledge inacces-
sible to the patient, and it is interesting to consider the ways
in which the profession has responded to this development.

The introduction of self-help groups has by no means been
greeted with open arms by the medical profession. Several groups,
both within the Women's Liberation Movement and outside it now
exist to help women understand, diagnose and treat minor gynaecological problems and urino-genital infections. It is these groups
which have introduced unconventional 'natural' treatments such as
the use of yoghourt in treating thrush. In the light of these
developments, a recent article on the medical page of a top selling
British women's magazine, by 'A Doctor' (Wimpole, 1976) is of
particular interest. While such articles frequently urge women, and
particularly mothers, not to bother doctors with minor troubles and
infections they can deal with themselves 'because your doctor is a
busy man', this particular article takes quite a different line.
Only 'a doctor' has the know-how to treat vaginal infections. The
article ends: 'immediate diagnosis is not all that easy. But
symptoms are often easy to put right once the *true* diagnosis has
been made, based upon a proper examination and simple tests by a
doctor' (our emphasis). More interesting perhaps is the discussion
of patients' self-diagnoses. This is clearly something to be
discouraged. The patient may make polite suggestions, but to
diagnose is overstepping the mark:

'I've got cystitis again,' or 'These antibiotics have given me
thrush', are phrases I hear every day. And these diagnoses are
often very wrong. What the girl *should* say is 'My urine hurts
and I keep wanting to go all the time,' or 'I've got an itchy
discharge. Do you think it might be caused by the Tetracycline
you gave me for that throat infection last week?' (our emphasis)

It might well be suggested that whereas in the past, doctors
maintained a certain control by refusing adequate treatment of
vaginal infections, failing to do adequate tests and so on, now that
women are developing their own means to deal with these infections,
doctors are able to say that only they, in their trained professional capacities, have the facilities and intelligence to deal with
such complaints.

We have argued above, and have supported the argument with preliminary findings from our research, that the relationship between
the GP and the patient contains aspects of control and power and
that this is particularly acute in the case of the large numbers of
middle-aged women who attend the surgery. In this context we
should note that the high consultation rates for all women, and
particularly for middle-aged women, reflect the various frustrations
of the life of a housebound woman. Our own findings on this
question corresponded with those of the study undertaken by
Wadsworth et al. (1971), who reported succinctly that 'Persons
complaining of headaches were significantly more likely to have
gone to a doctor if they were retired ... or housewives,... or
unemployed' (p.55).

It is important to make the connection between high consultation
rates and what is commonly regarded as a relatively unrewarding and

unabsorbing lifestyle. Housewives, although performing an economically, politically and socially essential task, have been encouraged to see themselves as isolated from the crucial functions of
production and the government of society. The consequence of this
isolation and sense of purposelessness (so well described in
Friedan's 'The Feminine Mystique', 1972) is that vulnerable women
turn frequently to their local GP for help and support. This is
especially true of women experiencing the crisis produced by children leaving home and the concurrent onset of the menopause. For a
woman with no life outside the home this can be a very dispiriting
and difficult time. The last thing she needs is reinforcement of a
sense of personal failure.

NOTES

1 Supported by the SSRC under the project title 'Women and Their
   Doctors: a Sociological Analysis of Consulting Rates'. The
   present paper is a preliminary discussion of the findings which
   will be published in full at a later date. The study is a small
   scale qualitative one, using 10 practices in different parts of
   the country. In each practice records are analysed, the GP
   interviewed and observed at some length, ancillary staff are
   observed and a sample of women patients interviewed. The sample
   is drawn from the 45-55 years age group and consists for each
   practice of 10 high and 10 low consulters.
2 The National Morbidity Survey provides a basis on which we have
   compared our respondents' practices with the national average.
3 Although sociology and community medicine are now taught in
   medical schools, the curriculum is still largely based on
   individual pathology.
4 Skultans' (1975) discussion of spiritualist practice provides an
   interesting parallel case.

4 Who needs prostitutes?
The ideology of male sexual needs

Mary McIntosh

The question of prostitution is usually treated as a moral one.
People argue that it is a wicked sin for a woman to prostitute
herself - or else that it is quite understandable as a way of making
a living, since men are willing to pay; people argue that men should
exercise moral restraint and confine sex to marriage - or else that
it is perfectly natural, especially if they are unmarried or away
from home, that they should seek release with a prostitute. A
common view, that of the 'double standard' of sexual morality, is
that frequenting prostitutes, perhaps more than other forms of
promiscuity, is forgivable in the male while being a prostitute,
again perhaps more than other forms of promiscuity, is totally
reprehensible in the female. What is seldom questioned is that it
is men who must resist or indulge their sexual urges while women
must resist or exploit the possibility of using their sexual
attractiveness for profit. It is taken for granted on all sides in
the moral debate that men 'demand' sex and women 'supply' it.
 Even Kingsley Davis (1937), in an article that represents a
genuine attempt to overcome ideology in the sociology of prostitution and that recognises that the institution of marriage and the
social dominance of men provide the main conditions for the
prostitution of women to men, falls back on a further justification
for his claim that prostitution is a universal phenomenon:
> Not only will there be a set of reproductive institutions which
> place a check upon sexual liberty, a system of social dominance
> which gives a motive for selling sexual favours, and a scale of
> attractiveness which creates the need for buying these favours,
> but prostitution is, in the last analysis, economical. Enabling
> a small number of women to take care of the needs of a large
> number of men, it is the most convenient sexual outlet for an
> army, and for the legions of strangers, perverts, and physically
> repulsive in our midst. (1937, p.755)

In a similar vein, Henriques (1968, p.315) suggests that there is an
irreducible 'hard core of demand' for prostitutes' services from
(a) the diseased, malformed and abnormal, (b) adolescents, and (c)
sailors and soldiers. This argument is a very curious one and is
only understood when it is seen as the last ditch into which the
defenders have been pushed by the supposed advance of 'permissiveness',

sex relations for mutual pleasure, or what is often bizarrely
called 'competition from amateurs'. Many men are now able to
satisfy their sexual 'needs' with partners who do not ask for
money payment. This was not possible for many in the nineteenth
and early twentieth centuries - indeed the revised edition of
Davis's article published in 1961 shows a much greater concern to
come to terms with the impact of sex freedom than the original did
in 1937. Where, in these liberated days, does the demand come from?

> On the one hand, the demand is the result of a simple biological
> appetite. When all other sources of gratification fail, due to
> defects of person or circumstance, prostitution can be relied
> upon to furnish relief. None of the exacting requirements of
> sex attraction and courtship are necessary. All that is needed
> is the cash. ... But in addition to the sheer desire for sexual
> satisfaction, there is the desire for satisfaction in a particu-
> lar (often unsanctioned) way. (Davis, 1937, p.753)

As Ernest Jones put it, 'in a large number of typical cases
potency is incompatible with marital fidelity, and can only be
achieved at the cost of adultery' (Jones, 1923, p.575, quoted
Thomas 1959, p.208). Prostitution, then, caters for different
people and different tastes that cannot be satisfied in marriage
or in sex freedom.

It is good that Davis recognises that sexual experiences are not
uniform interchangeable units. For most purposes it is not useful
to talk in terms of a 'total sexual outlet', derived from a variety
of 'sources', as Kinsey and his associates did (1948, 1953).
Certainly prostitution cannot be understood with a purely hydraulic
model as this would imply. Indeed, some clients do not ask for
anything that Kinsey would recognise as sexual and, according to
Stein (1974), most get a great deal of non-sexual 'psychotherapy'
from their encounters.

But where Davis really departs from the strictly sociological
analysis of most of the paper is in having recourse to a supposed
biological difference between men and women, rather than the social
one of relative power.

Innately, it seems, women have sexual attractiveness while men
have sexual urges. Prostitution is there for the needs of the male
hunchback - no one asks how the female hunchback manages. Havelock
Ellis (1936, pp.296f) is concerned about the needs of married men
with frigid wives, or who find 'a mysterious craving for variety',
or who are 'sexually perverted' with fetishistic cravings and about
men who seek the company of prostitutes because their style of life
is excitingly different from the women in their own social circle.
No one worries about the needs of women who might have these
'cravings' and desires. Thus does Ellis, a realist in sexual
matters, dismiss the suggestion of the moralists that the contradiction of prostitution could be resolved by early marriage and by
sexual restraint on the part of men to match that of women.

Ellis's monumental research on the sexuality of his day made him
aware that many men had such cravings whereas women on the whole
did not. The cravings of men constitute, as we have suggested, the
overt, socially recognised problem. Men consciously experience and
express sexual 'needs' that go beyond monogamy. In analyses such
as these, the observable 'needs' are taken as the determinants of

social institutions. The idea that there might be female sexual
'needs' that are repressed before they are expressed, or the idea
that the male needs are themselves socially produced, would be considered unscientific because they depend on things that cannot be
directly observed.

The empiricist approach collates its 'data' and concludes that
male sexuality is fundamentally different from female sexuality.
The male sexual urge is seen as being more imperious, more spontaneous, more specifically genital in goal, but also as being aroused
by objects and fantasies. The female urge is weaker, responds to
approaches from a partner, is more dependent upon the entire
relationship with the partner, yet the woman requires more direct
physical stimulation to reach orgasm.

The aim of this article is to question this empiricist formulation of male-female differences and to show that it is related to a
specific social ideology. It will not undertake the further, more
important and more difficult, task of developing a theory that
would be adequate to characterising and explaining the phenomena
in question.

The difference assumed by Davis and the others undoubtedly
correspond to our everyday beliefs and to many of our everyday
experiences of our own sexuality and that of other people. People
who do not fit the stereotype tend to be treated as abnormal. Men
who do not feel impulses towards sex for its own sake or who do not
care for erotic fantasies are despised. Women for whom sex is not
subordinated to a relationship are treated much more harshly. In
adolescence they are hounded by police and social workers for being
in 'moral danger' or 'sexually delinquent'. In some age groups the
behaviour most likely to get you in trouble with the police is
'sexual delinquency' (Cowie et al., 1968, p.191), behaviour which
is often acceptable for boys or for older people. In adulthood
promiscuous women can attract the attention of psychiatrists and
become labelled as 'nymphomaniacs'.

We often take these everyday beliefs and experiences as evidence
about the eternal nature of differences between the sexes. Sex,
after all, is something we think of as very 'natural' – you do it
with little or no equipment and with no clothes on. But nothing
could be further from the truth. There may be a generic 'sex'
drive that is natural, but the specific ways in which it will be
expressed, and indeed whether these will be recognisably 'sexual' at
all, depends upon the way in which the individual handles the general culture and the specific life-experiences she confronts. Thus
while careful scientific observers such as Kinsey, Masters and
Johnson and their colleagues may record differences in behaviour
and response that exist among mid-century Americans, they cannot
tell us, about the 'Human Male' the 'Human Female' or 'Human Sexual
Response' as they purport to.

Simone de Beauvoir has pointed out that:
The tremendous advance accomplished by psychoanalysis over
psychophysiology lies in the view that no factor becomes involved
in the psychic life without having taken on human significance;
it is not the body-object described by biologists that actually
exists, but the body as lived in by the subject. Woman is a
female to the extent that she feels herself as such. There are

biologically essential features that are not a part of her real,
experienced situation: thus the structure of the egg is not
reflected in it, but on the contrary an organ of no great biological importance, like the clitoris, plays in it a part of the
first rank. It is not nature that defines woman; it is she who
defines herself by dealing with nature on her own account in her
emotional life. (1972, p.69)

Simon and Gagnon go so far as rejecting the biological basis of
sexuality as to claim that:

Sexual behaviour is socially scripted behaviour and not the
masked or rationalised expression of some primordial drive. The
individual learns to be sexual as he or she learns sexual scripts,
scripts that invest actors and situations with erotic content.
(1969, p.736)

We need not go all the way with Simon and Gagnon to recognise that
even the most objective observations made in any given culture can
tell us only about the outcome of the patterns of response and motivation common in that culture. These are based, no doubt, on
biological structures, and on generic drives, but they are not the
same thing and they are not determined by them. We cannot assess
the full range of the sexual potentialities of women or of men by
looking at what they have done in the past or what they do in the
present, any more than we can assess the artistic or scientific
potentialities of women, or of men, by the same means.

Nevertheless, evidence from a variety of cultures can at least
demonstrate that the contemporary patterns of male and female
sexuality are far from universal (Ford and Beach, 1951; Oakley,
1972, pp.99ff). In many societies, such as the Arapesh described
by Margaret Mead (1935), men fear rape by women as much as women
fear rape by men in our society. The dominant, seductive female,
more highly sexed than the male, has even appeared from time to time
within the predominantly patriarchal Western Christian culture, in
what G. Rattray Taylor (1965) calls 'matrist' phases, like the
Renaissance, and also in the pre-Christian Celtic period (pp.32 and
149).

Steven Marcus (1966, pp.12ff) analyses with great subtlety the
system of beliefs underlying the supposedly scientific writing of
William Acton on 'The Function and Disorders of the Reproductive
Organs' (1857). He points out that the book was largely about male
sexuality, with female sexuality discussed only in relation to the
male. Acton's famous statement that 'the majority of women
(happily for them) are not very much troubled with sexual feeling
of any kind' was made in order to show young men that in marriage
they would find that sexual restraint was easier because a wife
would not display the strong (or apparently strong) passions of
'loose, or at least, low and vulgar women'. 'The best mothers,
wives and managers of households, know little or nothing of sexual
indulgences. Love of home, children and domestic duties, are the
only passions they feel.' Marcus points out that the underlying
belief is that

'sex is a curse and a torture, and the only hope of salvation for
men lies in marriage to a woman who has no sexual desires and who
will therefore make no sexual demands on her husband ... sexual
responsibility is being projected onto the role woman; she is

being required to save man from himself; and conversely if she
is by some accident endowed with a strongly responsive nature,
she will become the agent of her husband's ruin.' (p.32)
Marcus reveals many of Acton's apparently scientific statements to
be instances of 'ideology – that is of thought which is socially
determined yet unconscious of its determination' (p.30).

In the contemporary field of 'sex research' ideas are produced in
a somewhat less ideological, more scientific, way. Statements, such
as Acton's that women experience no great sexual excitement during
pregnancy or lactation, which Marcus characterised as part of a
wish-fulfilment fantasy, would nowadays not be allowed to pass
without being subjected to detailed and exhaustive empirical check-
ing (and, in this case, disproof). It is for this reason that the
work of such researchers is often described as scientific. In fact,
though, it is not strictly scientific since its problematic is one
of medical and social problems and its concepts are developed in
relation to these rather than to scientific problems. No proper
analysis has been done of the way in which knowledge in this field
is produced, but it is at least possible to point to examples of
outcomes that bear the stamp of ideology.

One of the most perceptive writers in this vein is Ruth Herschberger (1970), who, despite the fact that she wrote not only before
the giant research reports of Kinsey and his colleagues (1948, 1953)
and of Masters and Johnson (1966) but also before Simone de Beauvoir
(1949) provided the most general statement of the nature of the
ideology that deforms the scientific knowledge. In a devastatingly
witty essay criticising Yerkes's reports of his pioneering research
on chimpanzees' sexuality (especially Yerkes, 1943), she shows how
the words used in interpreting the observations make the findings
appear to confirm the cultural assumptions about basic differences
between male and female. In one experiment, for instance, Yerkes
had a male and a female chimpanzee in a cage and for a period of
thirty-two days observed which of them would get the food that came
down a chute at regular intervals. For eighteen days the male got
it and for fourteen days (while she was on heat) the female got it.
Yerkes wrote:

> When the female is not sexually receptive the naturally more
> dominant member of the pair almost regularly obtains the food;
> whereas during the female's phase of maximum genital swelling,
> when she is sexually receptive, she claims or may claim the food
> and take it regularly even though she be the naturally subordin-
> ate member of the pair. (1943)

Herschberger depicts the female chimpanzee's protests:

> Those words look like somebody decided I was subordinate way in
> advance.... There are sinister implications in this, for human
> females as well as for the women in our colony. If the period
> of sexual interest is, by implication, an extra-natural phase in
> women (it makes us *act* dominant when we're naturally subordinate),
> it looks like we girl chimps spend about 14 days out of every 32
> in the toils of Satan.... Besides, why call me sexually receptive
> anyway? That's one of those human words with an opinion written
> all over it. Call me sexually interested if you will, for I am.
> ... Receptive? I'm about as receptive as a lion waiting to be
> fed! (1970, pp.8-9)

Yerkes also claimed to have evidence of the 'biological basis of prostitution of sexual function' saying that the 'mature and sexually experienced female trades upon her ability to satisfy the sexual urge of the male' when she made a sexual invitation and later obtained the chute. Yet when the male made sexual invitations in the same circumstances, it was not reported as an attempt to trade.

The same kind of thinking was to be found in the Kinsey Reports. For example:

> A considerable proportion of the males in our sample who had had the opportunity to observe other persons in sexual activity had responded sympathetically during their observation. The females in the sample ... rarely reported such sympathetic responses. Most of them had been indifferent in their responses, if they had not been offended by the social impropriety of such an exhibition. It is, *therefore*, no accident, and not merely the product of the cultural tradition, that commercialised exhibitions of sexual activity, since the days of ancient Rome, have been provided for male but almost never for female audiences. (Kinsey et al., 1953, p.661)

This area of discussion is very important to the Kinsey conclusions, for they argue that 'there are fundamental psychologic differences between the two sexes' (p.574), whereas, 'in spite of the widespread and oft-repeated emphasis on the supposed differences between female and male sexuality, we fail to find any anatomic or physiologic basis for such differences' (p.641). The main 'psychologic' differences that they point to are that:

> The sexual responses and behaviour of the average male are, on the whole, more often determined by the male's previous experience, by his association with objects that were connected with his previous experience, by his vicarious sharing of another individual's sexual experience and by his sympathetic reactions to the sexual responses of other individuals. The average female is less often affected by such psychologic factors. It is highly significant to find that there are evidences of such differences between the males and females of infra-human mammalian species, as well as between human females and males. (p.650)

They admit that their differences offer an explanation of only 'some of the differences that we have reported in the incidences and frequencies of the patterns of sexual behaviour among females and males' and that 'there is tremendous individual variation' (p.650). Nevertheless they give great importance to the interpretation that 'in general, males are most often conditioned by their sexual experience and by a greater variety of associated factors, than females'. Yet when we examine the evidence that this is a 'psychologic' difference between men and women, it is very weak. The 'infra-human mammalian' argument is, of course, absurd. A few pages earlier they had noted that while males of other species often develop strong preferences for particular females, estrual females of sub-primate species almost never show such preferences - yet the pattern among humans today is, if anything, the reverse. Apparently, if we resemble other species it shows something deeply ingrained, if we differ it shows something uniquely, and perhaps also deeply, human.

The argument from the evidence about humans is not much better. The kind of figures Kinsey and his colleagues present (to choose a case where the male/female differences are considerable) are as shown in Table 4.1.

TABLE 4.1   Observing portrayals of sexual action

Erotic response	By females %	By males %
Definite and/or frequent	14	42
Some response	18	35
Never	68	23
Number of cases	2242	3868

Their comment is:

Many females, of course, report that they are offended by portrayals of sexual action, and denounce them on moral, social and aesthetic grounds. This is ordinarily taken as evidence of the female's greater sense of propriety; but in the light of our other data on the relative significance of psychologic stimulation for females and for males, it seems more likely that most females are indifferent or antagonistic to the existence of such material because it means nothing to them erotically. (p.662)

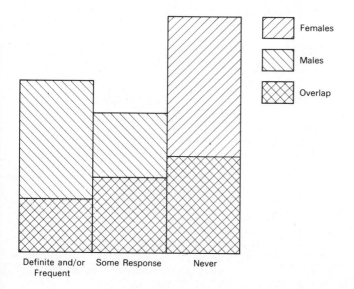

Definite and/or   Some Response   Never
Frequent

FIGURE 2   Observing portrayals of sexual action

The 'other data' are of exactly the same kind as this (pp.651-87),
and thus do nothing to reinforce the interpretation of the differences as due to 'fundamental' sex-linked 'psychologic' factors
rather than a culturally induced 'greater sense of propriety' in
women.   The differences in response are in any case not nearly as
great as the interpretations imply and certainly not great enough to
explain the variations in sexual activity patterns or justify
moralistic expectations.   If, instead of noting how the 'average'
or 'typical' (Kinsey and his colleagues eschew 'normal'; popular-
izers have not been so scrupulous) woman differs from the average or
typical man, we note instead how many men and women are *similar* we
find that there is a remarkable degree of overlap.   This is clear if
we present the earlier table as a diagram (see figure 2).   Fifty-
five per cent of women are matched by men who have the same response
- or lack of response - pattern.   For most of the other stimuli, the
overlap is very much greater (see Table 4.2).

TABLE 4.2   Overlap of response-pattern between sexes

Action	Overlap %
Observing the opposite sex	85
Observing one's own sex	96
Observing portrayals of nude figures	58
Observing own genitalia	53
Observing commercial moving pictures	88
Observing burlesque and floor-shows	52
Observing portrayals of sexual action	55
Observing animals in coitus	84
Preference for light or dark during coitus	79
Fantasies concerning opposite sex	85
Fantasies during masturbation	75
Reading literary materials	94
Erotic stories	67
Sado-masochistic stories	90
Being bitten	90

The two that have a lower overlap are not very surprising: male
genitalia are more impressive and easier to observe when tumescent;
strippers' acts are designed to appeal to heterosexual males rather
than to any females in the audience.   The only 'psychologic'
stimulus that erotically affects more women than men is 'observing
commercial moving pictures', which in Kinsey's day sometimes
included 'love scenes, close-ups of petting and kissing, and ...
exhibitionistic displays of semi-nude bodies'.   They cannot explain

this satisfactorily and certainly do not confront the challenge it
offers to their theory of 'fundamental psychologic differences
between the two sexes'. An explanation in cultural terms is, of
course, very easy.

So much for the 'science' of the pioneer sex researchers. But in
dismissing their interpretations, we should not throw out altogether
what can be gleaned from their observations. There *are* differences
between female and male sexuality in modern societies (Maccoby, 1966),
though some of these differences vary greatly within different
segments of the population (Kinsey, 1953, p.685) and at different
ages (which may perhaps be affected by hormonal factors - Kinsey,
1953, ch.18; Young, Goy and Phoenix, 1964). However, the fact that
men (now) *have* more sex does not mean they (always and everywhere)
need more sex.

Perhaps the most remarkable of the Kinsey conclusions (yet one
that evoked little comment at the time) was the rejection of any
anatomical or physiological basis for differences between male and
female sexuality. Fundamental differences did exist, he thought,
underlying the observed behavioural differences, but these were
psychological rather than anatomical or physiological. It was this
finding of Kinsey that led on to Masters and Johnson's more detailed
observational study of human sexual response (especially Masters and
Johnson, 1966). They charted the sexual-response cycles of men and
women and showed that they could be divided into the same four
phases of excitement, plateau, orgasm and resolution, though the
male orgasm was usually briefer and involved more intense contrac-
tions. They demonstrated the homology between the male and female
genital structures and the fact that it is the clitoris (of which
the male penis is the homologue) and not the vagina itself that is
sensitive to stimulation whether direct or during intercourse. They
showed that, when appropriately stimulated, women are usually
capable of a long series of orgasms.

Following from this research, Sherfey (1972) has argued that
biology gives to women an inordinate sexual drive and capacity
which had to be suppressed with the rise of modern civilisation, in
the interests of maternal responsibility and male property rights.
And Fisher (1973) has emphasised another aspect of the remoteness
of lived sexual experience from the biological basis by pointing out
that even though there are not two physically distinguishable
orgasms - the vaginal and the clitoral - yet women feel the results
of clitoral and vaginal stimulation to be very different, using
typically different adjectives and imagery to describe the resulting
orgasms (see also Glenn and Kaplan, 1968). We may add that for
both men and women the felt experience of orgasms which may be
physiologically identical will vary with the circumstances, fantasy,
relationship with the partner and so on.

In some of its popularisations the Masters and Johnson work has
led to biological reductionism, with the vaginal orgasm a 'myth'
because it has no biological basis and the solution to sexual
problems being seen in terms of improved stimulatory technique.
The writings of Sherfey and of Fisher, however, suggest a different
interpretation: that the nature of contemporary female (and presumably male) sexuality cannot be derived from the biological givens
and that we must look elsewhere both to characterise differences in

sexuality and to explain them.

The difficulty of thinking clearly in this area is compounded by the fact that the characteristics most common to men or to women become socially identified as 'masculine' or 'feminine' traits. Thus the psychiatrist Anthony Storr can write:

It is probably true that men are generally more 'sadistic' and women more 'masochistic'(1).... Women who do have truly sadistic desires are more commonly identifying themselves with men, and, if they act upon such feelings will therefore generally experience them in terms of a Lesbian relationship. (1964, pp.44-5)

Though it may be true that where dominance - or activity, autonomy, impersonality, rationality or anything else - are culturally associated with masculinity, a sadistic woman will tend to identify with 'men', Storr's implicit assumption that dominance and so forth are absolutely male is mistaken. Sigmund Freud referred to this as the 'error of superimposition' (1973, p.148) and wrote:

It is essential to realize that the concepts of 'masculine' and 'feminine', whose meaning seems unambiguous to ordinary people, are among the most confused to occur in science.... Every individual ... displays a mixture of the character-traits belonging to his own and the opposite sex; and he shows a combination of activity and passivity whether or not these last character-traits correspond with his biological ones. (Freud, 1905, pp.219-20)

Using the terms 'belonging' and 'correspond' in the very same passage, Freud shows himself unable to shed the assumptions of 'ordinary people'. These assumptions are part of a deep-seated and elaborate ideology that has so often guided the work of the sex researchers and this is articulated in a mystifying everyday language in which it is all but impossible to avoid mistakes of this kind.

The differences between men and women that do exist are developed in relation to this same ideology. But they are also developed in the life experiences of women and men. Boys and young men can engage in a wider variety of sexual activities because they are freer and less closely supervised; young women treat sex itself as less significant than the overall relationship because, for them, it is very important to get married as they need a man to depend on financially as well as emotionally. It is women's socio-economic dependence, as Davis pointed out, that leads them to 'use' sex as a means to an end rather than treat it as an end in itself. The more active sexuality of men, positively seeking pleasure and achievement, is but a part of the general dominance of men over women and a part of the wider social situation in which man is cast as the Subject, the Absolute, and woman as the Object, the Other (de Beauvoir, 1972). She is passive, responsive only to his initiatives, because he is the dominant partner. Similarly, the greater strength and frequency of the male urge is an aspect of male privilege, just as *gourmandise* or a taste for Meissen vases is an aspect of class privilege.

Thus the ideology is not only purveyed in churches, classrooms, newspapers, and over garden fences; it is not only enforced through the law on prostitution, divorce, rape, child-custody; it is also embodied in attitudes that are appropriate to the positions and

relations that people find themselves in. The ideology of sexuality
has a material basis, and its basis is, of course, the division
between men and women as this is organised through the monogamous
'patriarchal' family.

   In men there tends to be a much greater elaboration of the
physical aspects of sex. As Kinsey noted, the partner's appearance,
erotica and pornography, sexual fantasy and objects associated with
coitus, more often play an important role in men's sexuality. In
women it is more often the relational aspect that has become elaborated. Women have 'sexual relationships' whereas men engage in 'sex
acts'. Herschberger (1970, p.17) has suggested that this is an
important element in 'the myth of rape' and this is also why we find
it much easier to 'understand' a male gigolo than a female prostitute. How can she engage in a sexual relationship with all-and-
sundry and without emotion?, we ask. There is something unfeminine
about it. Yet for a man to frequent prostitutes is certainly not
unmanly.

   The moral rule associated with this greater elaboration of the
relational aspect is 'the double standard'. The opinion, often a
fact, that Byron expressed as:

    Man's love is of man's life a thing apart,
    'Tis woman's whole existence.

justifies the view that unchastity is much more evil in woman than
in a man. For a man, it is simply giving in to his sexual urge; for
a woman, it is a betrayal of her husband or father and of her whole
home and family life. The Victorians believed that prostitution
kept *homes* pure by keeping women pure; the promiscuity of the menfolk apparently did not sully the domestic hearth.

Keith Thomas has argued that:

    the English insistence on female chastity cannot be explained by
    reference to the fact of childbirth and elaborations thereon, but
    that the solution is more likely to be found in the desire of men
    for absolute property in women. (1959, p.216)

Whichever is the explanation, this area of sexual ideology and
sexual orientation is clearly associated with female monogamy, the
system in which each wife has one husband only, to whom she is subordinate. The system may have been stronger, and the ideology
stronger, in the nineteenth century but the view that pre-marital
and extra-marital sex relations are more acceptable for men than
for women is still held by some today (Gorer, 1973, ch.7).

   The question of differential sexuality, the question 'who wants
sex, and of what sort?' can thus be seen as a sociological and not a
biological one. Its answer is rooted in specific social structures.
The ideology of male sexual needs both supports and is supported by
the structures of male dominance, male privilege and monogamy.

   But demonstrating that a system of ideas, in its various manifestations, is an ideology and that it is appropriate to a social
structure is only the beginning. What remains to be done, and
cannot be attempted here, is to show how the ideology is produced
and reproduced. Partly this is accomplished through feedback
mechanisms such as we find in prostitution: the way that the idea of
male sexual needs supports institutionalised female prostitution is
obvious; not so obvious perhaps is the way that prostitution reinforces that ideology. Yet the existence of female and not male

prostitution must to some extent bolster the idea that women do not
need sex enough to demand it in the market and that men need it
enough to be willing to pay dearly for it. Like rape, like contemporary forms of pornography, like beauty competitions, like much of
our public culture, prostitution contributes to the casting of woman
as object and man as subject, and thus to the prevailing ideology.
Yet feedback mechanisms can only be part of the story.
    Ruth Herschberger posed the problem in this way:
    It was quite a feat of nature to grant the small clitoris the
    same number of nerves as the penis. It was an even more incred-
    ible feat that society should actually have convinced the
    possessors of this organ that it was sexually inferior to the
    penis. (1970, pp.32-3)
Suffice to say that there are three types of answer to this problem.
The first is that of Gagnon and Simon (1974), mentioned earlier,
which suggests that sexual behaviour, like any other, is socially
scripted behaviour and if men and women behave differently it is
because the socially available scripts for them to learn are different. If they could be presented with a new script, their
patterns of behaviour would alter. The second type of answer is
that women's sexuality is suppressed (or, it is sometimes said,
repressed) by men or in the interests of patriarchy. Women are kept
in leading-strings by father, husband, Church and State, so that the
extent and range of their sexual expectations and opportunities is
limited and they are prevented from realising their full potential.
The third type of answer is the Freudian one, that the differentiation of sexuality, along with other orientations, occurs in the
history of each individual in an infancy in which mother and father
play specific different parts - in other words, in the Oedipal
situation. The advantage of the Freudian approach over the other
two is that it enables the theorisation of the specific differences
between men and women, whereas the scripting approach leaves the
content of the scripts as a contingent matter, and the suppression
approach sees women's sexuality in a purely negative and men's in a
purely positive light. There are many problems with Freud as well,
not least that in his own writings he often assigned an innate
superiority to the penis, seeing female penis envy as an inevitable
outcome of the anatomical difference, and he saw the Oedipus complex as a universal to be found in any civilised society. Modern
interpretations (for example, Mitchell, 1974) may be able to overcome
these without departing from Freud's basic principles, yet there
still remains the task of identifying variations in the Oedipal
situation in different types of society and specifying the social
conditions of its absence. Unlike the other two approaches,
Freudian theory at least provides the tools for starting on this
task.

NOTES

1 Since this statement is based on clinical experience, it should
   really read, 'more men are "sadistic" and more women are
   "masochistic"'.

5 Sexual codes and conduct
A study of teenage girls

Deirdre Wilson

This analysis is part of an ongoing research project which offers a feminist perspective on the field of women and deviance in sociology. Here, 'feminist perspective' is defined as an approach to sociological investigation which is primarily concerned with the belief systems and attitudes of girls and women, supported by an analysis of the social, economic and cultural forces which structure their lives, and with the way in which specific theories and ideas influence the evaluation and the structure of social relationships.

The empirical focus of the research is a participant observation study of the lives of two groups of girls in a Northern city, aged between thirteen and fifteen. A minority of these girls are officially described as delinquent, that is, they are evaluated as such by agents of formal social control. The remainder are often involved on the fringes of delinquency, in other words, they take part in acts which are at odds with legal and social norms, whether responded to or not by the agents of formal social control.

The two groups of girls might at any one time have had a maximum membership of nine, three or four of whom could be described as the core members. The areas of Riverside and Dockside, the neighbourhoods of the respective groups, were separated in the city by a narrow district where both the magistrates court and social services were situated.

Riverside, once a respectable middle-class residential area, became a notorious lodging-house and terraced area. There had been widespread development of high-rise flats and maisonettes over recent years and the whole remaining area was scheduled for redevelopment. Dockside had largely been cleared of old terraces, though a few streets remained under compulsory purchase orders. It became a major resettlement area of modern council property, although quite a number of families who originated from Riverside still held close associations with that area rather than Dockside.

Both districts had long been considered by residents of the city as a whole, as discrete traditional working-class neighbourhoods and both were renowned for a high delinquency and crime rate. This reputation persisted although the majority of the inhabitants were law-abiding citizens.

Within each district there were smaller territories and this

study was confined to one particular set of dwellings in each area
which constituted individual territories. These are referred to as
Palace Court and Grayson Place in Riverside and Dockside respect-
ively. These buildings served as meeting places for the girls
taking part in the study.

The delinquent activities in which the girls were involved were
predominantly petty shoplifting and persistent non-attendance at
school. They were also involved in, in the sense of having knowledge of, other delinquent activities by virtue of friendship with
groups of boys from the same areas. The pattern of the delinquent
behaviour of the girls in the study reflected the criminal statistics for the city as a whole, where only 3 per cent of all girls
brought before the local juvenile court in the period from April
1976 to October 1976, were for being 'beyond parental control' or
'in need of care and protection', whereas 40 per cent were brought
to court on charges of theft. There were no cases of girls being
charged with explicitly sexual misdemeanours. However, in practice,
the categories of being 'in need of care and protection' and 'beyond
control' were employed to deal with the sexual activities of young
girls. Consequently the number of girls considered to be 'beyond
control', expressed as a proportion of the total population of
female delinquents, was small, and therefore did not bear out the
prevailing idea among sociologists and society as a whole, that
'delinquent girls are sexual delinquents'.

This latter view has prevailed despite contrary contemporary
evidence (1) which shows that among female offenders forms of theft
greatly exceed sexual offences. The reasons why no revised description of female delinquency has emerged in sociology are complex.
The history of the sociology of deviance, as far as women and girls
are concerned, is an history of the uncritical adoption of conventional wisdom about the nature of women, namely that anatomy is
destiny. The predominance of certain theoretical orientations and
their effect on the form of explanation of female delinquency can
partially account for the emphasis in criminology on sexual deviance.

The social system/structural-functionalist approach emphasises
the influence of social structural features on individuals and
groups, as well as the differential structuring of opportunities
which may lead to deviance. When applied to delinquency the implic-
ation is that particular acts are related to, or rather are the
outcome of, the frustration of particular primary success goals, for
example, boys 'naturally' commit offences against property and girls
are involved in sexual delinquency. In analyses of this kind
'expected' forms of deviance are seen to originate in, or arise
from, the specific characteristics of the social location of the
deviants. In the case of men and boys the explanation is in terms
of their centrality to the occupational/financial syndrome, and for
women it is in terms of their sexual relations with men, the latter
being seen as the key components of the adult feminine role.
Cloward and Ohlin (1961) whose influence in guiding contemporary
research work in deviance has already been documented, (2) viewed
juvenile delinquency as primarily a means of gaining status in
certain environments. Here, culturally approved aspirations coupled
with limited possibilities of legitimately realising such aspirations, create a condition of strain which can result in delinquency

and the development of a subculture. This explanation of deviant
behaviour which was formulated to account for male delinquency has
been assumed to be appropriate to an understanding of female delinquency. The unjustified generalisation of this explanation,
primarily formulated in relation to male activity, reflects Simmel's
observation that in a masculine culture:

[masculine] is taken as the universal norm, applied equally to
the phenomena of individual masculine and of the individual
feminine ... [and where] expressions of masculinity are easily
elevated for us to the realm of supra-specific, neutral,
objectivity and validity. (Quoted in Klein, 1946, p.62)

In sociology, therefore, where male delinquency is understood as
role expressive, female delinquency is assumed to be synonymous
with sexual delinquency. In addition to this assumption about
female delinquency, the incorporation of explanations of female
deviance within a problematic constructed to account for male
deviance has effectively placed female delinquents on the margins
of sociological enquiry.

The female delinquent is often described as the 'lone' delinquent,
and therefore explanations of such delinquency must necessarily
focus on the 'personal'. This view is exemplified by the following
remark:

Almost invariably her problems are deeply personalised. What-
ever her offense - whether shoplifting, truancy or running away
from home - it is usually accompanied by some disturbance of
unfavourable behaviour in the sexual area. (Konopka, 1966, p.4)

It may be that traditional subcultural explanations of deviance
are not appropriate to female crime but for a different reason than
the fact that the expression of the feminine role is inappropriate in
a traditional masculine form of organisation. There is the possibility, as yet unexplored, that female delinquents are actually in
rebellion against or ambivalent to their ascribed feminine role.

This paper is an investigation into the attitudes of girls, both
officially defined and self-defined as delinquent, towards sexual
conduct; girls who are prepared to 'jeopardise' their feminine
status because of the symbolically masculine nature of the delinquency in which they engage.

Any investigation into the field of sexuality is difficult if
only because of the ambiguities in the notion of sexuality itself
and the even greater ambiguities as to what is meant by gender
appropriate or 'normal' sexuality. The concept of sexuality
adopted here was derived from what Morgan (1975) calls the interactional and transactional processes that take place within a
culture or subculture whereby a particular activity comes to be
defined by the participants as sexual. In what follows, the definition of sexuality, as expressed in sexual conduct, is that belonging to the girls who took part in the study. Sexuality is defined
in terms of a male/female relationship under certain conditions,
and although a few very intense dyadic friendships existed between
girls, which if heterosexual would probably have led to sexual
involvement, there was no evidence of any lesbian involvement.

During the course of the research it became apparent that there
existed certain rules which governed the expression of sexuality in
sexual conduct. Whyte's Slum Sex Code (1943) elaborated the

differential aspects of respect and responsibility accorded to girls
who were categorised by the street-corner boys of his study in terms
of their willingness to engage in pre-marital sex. But he presents
his analysis of sexual behaviour and attitudes in the 'slums' without any reference to the girls concerned and with very little reference to the traditional sexual mores of the district. This paper
presents an alternative view, focusing on a sex code sustained by
the interaction amongst the girls themselves, with the 'assistance'
of the neighbourhood boys, their families, and the agents of formal
social control. By a code is meant a set of implicit rules which
constitute guidelines for the girls' behaviour involving not only
definitions of different categories of boys, but also a system of
self-classification. Basically, for the girls these rules govern
whom to have sex with and under what circumstances. The code constitutes a middle ground between the promiscuity which appears to be
advocated by the 'permissive society', and the ideal of virginity
advocated by official agencies, and to a large degree, the families.

Whom to have sex with and when initially depends on the nature
of a girl's self-image. Whyte's classification was originally
adopted in this project, but the girls expressed disagreement over
the relevance of Whyte's categories, over the appropriateness of
them to their own behaviour and self-images. The majority of the
girls resented the narrow conception of 'good girls' in Whyte's
schema, particularly in so far as it, by definition, excluded any
girl who had actively expressed, or was actively expressing her
sexuality. As a result a different classification was constructed
based on the girls' own conceptions of themselves and of each
other. Interestingly the categories which emerged were not
coterminous with the 'good girls'/'lays' distinction of Whyte's
study. The typology shown in Table 5.1 only refers to those girls
involved in the present study, twenty girls aged between thirteen
and seventeen years.

TABLE 5.1 Comparison of girls' categories and Whyte's categories
of female sexuality

Girls' typology		Whyte's typology
Classification	Number of girls	Classification
I Virgins (not out of choice)	3	I Good girls (virgins)
II Virgins (out of choice)	4	
III One-man girls	11	II Lays a) One-man girls
IV Lays (Whyte's promiscuous)	2	b) Promiscuous c) Prostitutes
Total	20	

Most of the girls defined themselves as 'one-man' girls but this category may be misleading. The regularity of the girls' sexual activity was always governed by opportunity and an element of risk. In effect, the 'one-man' girls had sex with one boy during any one period about twice a week, maybe less. Those who were not actively involved in 'carrying out' the rules of the code, nevertheless were aware of the restrictions on their behaviour should they have wished to begin their sexual careers. Those girls who were virgins, but 'not out of choice', were the girls who were waiting for the right boy to come along and fully intended to lose their virginity before they got married. Those who were virgins 'out of choice' were usually too young to consider being involved in sexual relationships, but also there were two girls who did not want to become involved because of a fear of the consequences, either discovery by their parents, or of pregnancy. Those girls who were defined as 'lays' will be considered below as they appeared to reject one of the basic rules of sexual conduct.

CLASSIFICATION OF BOYS

The girls operated with a three-way classification of the boys in their neighbourhoods. These were as follows:
  I Untouchables - usually the homely type, or those boys considered to be under the influence of their mother.
 II Nice boys - these constituted the type of boys a girl would aim
    for, the future steady boyfriend.
III Boasters - these would tell everyone in the neighbourhood if
    they had had sex with a girl, irrespective of the kind of girl
    she was. He often had more than one girl 'on the go' at any
    one time and was an equivalent in some respects to the girls
    defined as 'lays'.
The 'nice' boys were by far the most numerous, according to the girls,
    'They treat you nice, they don't go telling all your friends
    about whether or not you've been with them.... I suppose they
    (the boys) do talk but you never get any lip from his mates
    even if he does tell them anything ... they're the ones you'd
    like to marry.'
As a rule, the nice boys were the ones a girl got involved with. When asked at what point in the relationship the question of sexual involvement arose, the girls usually answered 'when you're going steady with him of course, if he asks you before then he's no good.'
The question of what constituted a steady as opposed to a casual relationship seemed, in the girls' terms, to be fairly well defined. The seriousness of a relationship increased as the boy and girl saw more of each other without any of their friends, although once a steady relationship had been formed, it was not uncommon for each partner to re-enter their former friendship groups. Casual friendships occurred where groups were involved, the boys and girls arrived at youth clubs and parties in groups and left in groups. Whyte emphasised the significance of his boys visiting the girl's home, interpreting it as a sign of an unofficial engagement. Such visits were not of the same importance in either Palace Court or

Grayson Place. Boys and girls frequently entered each others'
homes from an early age and no special significance was attached to
these visits.

A steady relationship usually developed from an initial date
where the girl and boy were alone. Dates by themselves, however
many, did not constitute a steady relationship, even if the dates
persisted over a period of a few months. In asking the question
what made a steady relationship different from just a date, the
answer was: 'It's steady when you decide to make it steady ... he
usually says shall we go steady and you say yes or no.' 'A steady
is serious, it means you love him....' Sexual involvement nearly
always followed this kind of commitment to a change in the status of
the relationship, or else the two occurred simultaneously.

The fundamental rule governing sexual behaviour was the existence
of affection in the form of romantic love before any sexual commitment. For most of the girls, love existed before sex, and it was
never a consequence of sexual involvement. The high commitment to
marriage amongst working-class girls has been noted in previous
studies (Mungham, 1976) and the girls in this study also firmly
believed in marriage, and marriage at an early age. The majority of
girls thought it best to be married before twenty, and certainly
before twenty-one. Steady relationships which continued for over a
year, even if the girl was only fifteen, were often seen by the girl
herself and her friends as an informal engagement, because the
pattern of a steady teenage relationship followed by a marriage at
seventeen or eighteen already existed in the neighbourhood, and
often in the girls' own families.

Morgan (1975) suggests that sexual conduct is an area of social
behaviour which because of its prime focus on intensive dyadic
relationships, appears to possess and in some ways does possess a
greater degree of autonomy than perhaps many other areas of life.
Therefore, the presence of schemes of interaction which act to
sustain a certain code of behaviour and regulate deviations from
that code, begs the question as to what extent the girls in the
study were able to govern the expression of their own sexuality.

The girls regulated their contact with other girls who were
known as 'lays', in order to preserve their own reputations. In
fact they openly ridiculed the girls, referring to them as whores.
(3) The two girls in the study who classified themselves and were
only reluctantly classified by the others as 'lays', had at that
time crossed the socially constructed division between 'one-man'
girls and 'lays', and had both become involved in steady relationships. The others were reluctant to define these two girls as
'lays' partly because of the stigma attached to associating with
'bad girls' and partly because the two girls appeared reconciled to
the notion of romantic love, declaring that 'this time I really
love him and he loves me'. If, however, the steady relationship
should end the girl concerned may well be redefined as a 'lay' and
may ultimately drift away from the group. Such girls who come to
believe that sex may exist without love or marriage may still have
a commitment to the idea of eventual marriage comparable to other
girls. Amongst the girls in the study marriage was seen as the
natural step after school, and the job that they might take up in
between these stages in their life was seen as merely a way to pass
time.

Within these groups of girls, expressions of sexuality could only
receive support or be condoned when they maintained the triangular
relationship of love, sexuality and marriage. These three are
intricately related and the girls seemed unable to express sexuality
without the presence of love, which was in turn seen as a natural
and necessary precondition for marriage. Any deviation by a girl,
from what Reich (1970) has called the repressive triangle, resulted
in a rejection by her peers. This effectively meant that access to
her former social life was denied. But, given this threat of rejection, it was difficult to discover just how many girls *actually*
believed in the primacy of love, and how many simply paid lip
service to the ideal. Nevertheless, the fact that the girls found
it necessary to support this convention, whether they believed in it
or not, was an important fact in itself.
     It was not only the girls who decided on the sanctions to be
employed against deviant members. The boys also had their part to
play in the maintenance of the sexual mores of the neighbourhood
(that is, in controlling the sexual behaviour of the girls). This
was achieved in two ways; either by the boys appearing to support
the ideal of romantic love in order to convince the girls to have
sex with them without breaking their code of sexual conduct, or by
sanctioning those girls who freely admitted believing in sex without
love and who appeared to share the boys' instrumental attitude
towards sex. When a girl entered into a steady relationship but
refused to acknowledge that it might be permanent and when she
denied being in love with the boy, he would take the girl's lack of
commitment as a violation of the code that both the girls and the
boys were supposed to live by (*regardless* of whether the boy himself
saw the relationship as temporary and devoid of love). In such a
situation it was not unusual for the girl's name to be passed around
the school and streets as being easy. When this double standard of
morality was mentioned in the presence of the girls and boys (4)
however, the boys became very uncomfortable, maintaining that they
also abided by the code of sexual conduct and emphasising that they
could only have sex with girls they 'genuinely' liked. The existence of a double standard of sexual morality was however quite
apparent amongst the boys and the girls. The mere fact that the
girls divided themselves into separate groups based upon a definition of their sexual behaviour and the fact that so-called 'lays'
were excluded from group membership would emphasise this. Moreover,
while the girls were categorised in sexual terms by both the boys
and the girls, the boys themselves did not define each other in the
same way. That is to say, within the boys' groups there were no
equivalents to the 'lays' of the girls' groups and the 'promiscuous'
boy apparently did not suffer any loss of prestige or status. Nor
was it perceived as unusual for 'promiscuous' boys to mix freely
with others.
     The differential treatment of girls according to their respective
sexual statuses (as 'lays', 'one-man' girls or virgins) was reflected in the attitudes of both the girls' families and the more
formal agents of social control. In an area where illegitimate
births and forced marriages were commonplace, the girls who could
justify their sexual activities by reference to the inevitability of
marriage to the boys concerned, received fewer sanctions from their

families than those girls who had rejected the association of sex
with love and marriage. Often, these girls had rejected the influence of their parents and the legitimacy of the repressive triangle,
thereby creating strains within the family. This then resulted in
physical punishment which appeared to be a generalised sanction
against promiscuity, but which was more a reaction against the
flouting of the neighbourhood code of sexual conduct.

The courts and social welfare agencies tend to treat sexual
'promiscuity', on the part of teenage girls, as a very serious
matter. Indeed it has been shown that girl 'offenders' are treated
differentially according to whether or not they appear to have been
sexually active, and moreover one of the latent functions of the
juvenile court appears to be the reinforcement of the conventional
female sex role.(5) In a six-month period from April 1976 to
October 1976, observation of a juvenile court revealed that it was
often doubtful whether supervision orders made upon some girls, were
imposed on them as a result of the offence which had been committed,
as is the case with boys, or whether the orders were made because of
deviations from the expected form of feminine behaviour. It was
certainly not unusual for questions to be asked by the magistrates
concerning the moral welfare of female offenders, and the few orders
for 'care and protection' and for being 'beyond control' were all
concerned with sexual activities or rather the suspicion of sexual
activity. The posing of questions of this kind can only be understood by realising that female delinquency is generally assumed to
be synonymous with sexual delinquency. In contrast the sexual
behaviour of delinquent boys is generally considered to be immat-
erial by the courts.

In the traditional working-class areas of Riverside and Dockside,
teenage girls were faced with limited educational opportunities and
the prospect of dead-end jobs. The girls had a high commitment to
marriage at an early age, and social life in the area was family-
centred. Marriage not only provided the easiest and most obvious
means of escape from the parental home, but also signified the
transition into adulthood for the girls. It was essential therefore
for the girls to safeguard their entry into the mainstream of adult
social life - namely marriage - by adhering to the neighbourhood
code of sexual conduct. However, this code did not preclude all
forms of pre-marital sex, as the girls operated with a more highly
differentiated set of sexual mores than the basic virgin/whore
distinction. In consequence they were able to be actively sexual
without defining themselves either as 'bad' or as delinquent.
However, the forms in which they could legitimately express their
sexuality were limited and constrained, the control and legitimation
of the expressions of their sexuality being effectively achieved by
an adherence to the triangular ideology of love, sexuality and
marriage which they manipulated, consciously or otherwise, in their
social life.

NOTES

1 For evidence regarding crime statistice for England and Wales,
   see the Official Criminal Statistics, and also Davies and
   Goodman (1972).
2 The influence of Cloward and Ohlin is traced in an analysis of
   four sociological journals during the period 1940-70, by
   J. F. Galliher (1973).
3 The lack of solidarity among girls in regard to those who have a
   reputation for being 'easy' has been noted by McRobbie and
   Garber (1975). In this study, the majority of girls commonly
   engaged in making derogatory comments which reinforced their own
   status.
4 The boys who were present were the boyfriends of some of the
   girls who were also taking part in the discussion.
5 See M. Chesney-Lind (1973) and L. Shacklady Smith in this volume.

6 Sexist assumptions and female delinquency
An empirical investigation

Lesley Shacklady Smith

INTRODUCTION

Research into female delinquency has never attracted a great deal of
attention, either from professional criminologists or social administrators. The explanation for this lack of interest is not hard to
find - females having been conceptualised as less delinquent, less
dangerous and less involved in deviant subcultures than males (Cowie
et al., 1968), have thus rather naturally been seen as posing far
fewer social problems than adolescent males. Indeed nearly all
theorists have argued that the only areas where girls have posed
problems are those of sexual promiscuity and occasional shoplifting.
These are hardly the type of offences to arouse the interest of
criminologists and sociologists, and though from time to time moralists have expressed concern about the growing promiscuity of young
girls, significantly it was not until the 1971 crime statistics
revealed a more rapid increase in crimes of violence among females
than males that the media and a few psychologists started to
show a more direct concern in the growing number of female
delinquents.(1)

Even so, there still exists only a small body of writings specifically concerned with female delinquency. These writings, with a
few notable exceptions (Chesney-Lind, 1973; Hoffman-Bustamante, 1973;
Smart, 1976), tend to be highly moralistic in tone and based on
common-sense and sexist assumptions (Cowie et al., 1968; Thomas,
1967). Moreover, there has been little, if any, attempt to examine
the 'organisational activity' which produces the official rates of
female delinquency. According to one sociologist, 'our knowledge of
the character and causes of female criminality is at the same stage
of development that characterised our knowledge of male criminality
some 30 or more years ago' (Ward et al., 1969).

The present paper attempts to challenge some of the assumptions
present in previous research and examine the nature of female
delinquency from a more sociological perspective. It will be argued
that the idea that female delinquents are restricted in their
deviant behaviour is largely a consequence of weak statistical
analysis. This analysis in turn has led to most research workers in
the field being seduced by the simplistic appeal of biological and

psychiatric explanations, where the concepts of innate sexual differences, the defective personality, and bad home background have
been continually resorted to (Aldridge-Morris, 1968; Blos, 1957;
Cowie et al., 1968; Durea and Assum, 1948). An alternative approach
is suggested which not only treats the nature of female delinquency
as problematic, but sets out to show that a variety of offences are
hidden because of the way law-enforcing agencies, parents and social
workers tend to react to female deviants. I will also attempt to
show how social reaction to female deviancy has influenced the
pattern of female delinquency among a group of delinquent girls
studied in the Bristol area between 1969 and 1972.

SEXIST ASSUMPTIONS AND THE NATURE OF FEMALE DELINQUENCY

The predominant form of empirical research on the nature of female
delinquency published over the last ten years (Cowie et al., 1968;
Konopka, 1966; Vedder and Sommerville, 1970) owes a great deal to
the sexist assumptions inherent in the classical studies of female
criminality (cf. Lombroso and Ferrero, 1895; Pollak, 1961; Thomas,
1907). Despite recent critiques by Klein (1973) and Smart (1976)
the underlying sexism in the classical studies prevails in contemporary empirical research on the topic of female delinquency. A
brief examination of these sexist assumptions is given below.
   Since Lombroso and Ferrero (1895) female criminality has been
explained in terms of 'so-called' innate characteristics thereby
reconfirming and further reifying specific ideological assumptions
concerning the nature of femininity and the female sex. A recent
example of this is to be found in the work of Cowie et al. (1968)
who when analysing the differences between male and female delinquents state: 'Differences between the sexes in hereditary predis-
position [to crime] could be explained by sex-linked genes. Furthermore, the female mode of personality, more timid, more lacking in
enterprise, may guard her against delinquency' (p.167).
   Clearly Cowie et al., and other theorists who have adopted
similar positions, are making quite explicit assumptions about the
inherent nature of women. Since this 'nature' is seen as universal
there is no consideration of historical data or cross-cultural
studies which in fact reveal that there are many different modes of
'female personality'.
   Inherent, also, in such preconceptions about the 'female mode of
personality' is the belief that female delinquents must be far more
abnormal and pathological than their male counterparts. This is so,
or so the argument goes, because delinquency among girls is such a
perversion of or rebellion against their *natural* feminine roles
which stress passivity and conformity. As a result of this belief
there has arisen a variety of small-scale studies *all* indicating a
plethora of abnormal characteristics. These range from educational
retardation and very poor homes, to ungainly and masculine appearance, and deficient personalities. But the two factors pinpointed
as having most significance - broken homes and psychiatric disorders
- have consistently dominated theoretical attention, and have
resulted in a projection of the delinquent girl as a deprived and
inadequate individual. Deprived because she has neither the economic

security or emotional warmth a female needs for relational successes;
inadequate because she has failed to achieve the appearance of
passive female normality.

Another belief which has emanated from the assumed pathology of
female delinquents has been that such social factors as class,
societal reaction, subcultures and so on are largely irrelevant to
an understanding of the 'abnormal' female delinquent. Again, in the
words of Cowie et al. (1968) the prevailing ideology derived from
the classical studies has been that

> social factors have been found to be of very great importance in
> the causation of delinquency in boys, there is little evidence
> that they play anything like the same part in the case of girls.
> Subcultural delinquency seems not to have been explored at all in
> relation to girls. The effective motivational factors are con-
> nected, much more than with boys, with the intimate family and
> with the girls' personal relations with her parents. (p.44)

The contradiction inherent in statements like this is clear.
Social factors are dismissed not upon scientifically proven arguments which may show that the etiology of delinquency between the
sexes is different (2), but quite simply on the basis that since no
research has examined social factors they must be irrelevant. This,
of course, totally ignores the fact that the reason why researchers
have not worked within a more sociological framework is because of
their prior assumptions concerning the inherent differences between
the sexes, which in turn leads to the quite extreme conclusion that
while sociological variables may influence the male, the female
somehow lives in such an isolated environment that she is totally
immune to these factors. The way in which previous research has
started its analysis by accepting the validity of criminal and
delinquency statistics is also worth noting.(3)

This consequently leaves them the task of explaining the rather
undramatic fact as to why females restrict their delinquent activities to sexual misconduct and occasional shoplifting. Indeed to
most of these writers female delinquency can quite simply be equated
with sexual delinquency, which reifies their 'common-sense' assertion that 'it is more natural to suppose that the male-female
differences, both in delinquency rates and in the form delinquency
takes, would be closely connected with the masculine or feminine
pattern of development of personality' (Cowie et al., 1968, p.170).

This brief examination of the previous literature suggests four
important hypotheses that are in one way or another taken as assumed
facts. These are (a) female delinquency is largely restricted to
sexual delinquency, (b) female delinquents are seldom involved in
delinquent subcultures, (c) more sociological approaches, such as
that of the labelling approach, are not applicable to an understanding of female delinquency, (d) female delinquents are far more
abnormal and pathological than their male counterparts. My own
research was concerned with showing that each of these assumptions
was false and that an interactional framework was needed within
which the nature of female delinquency could be examined.

OBJECTIVES AND METHODOLOGY

As has been said, one of the aims of this paper is to show that
previous conceptualisations of female delinquency are inadequate.
The information presented here is the result of research I carried
out in the Bristol and Bath area between 1969 and 1972. The study
included:
  (a) an examination of the court case records of all girls between
      the ages 14-16 who were referred to the Bristol juvenile courts
      during 1969;
  (b) in-depth interviews with 30 girls who had received probation
      or supervision orders;(4)
  (c) in-depth interviews with 30 girls who had not been referred to
      any juvenile court or other agencies dealing with juvenile
      misconduct, with the necessary controls for social class,
      schools etc., who acted as a useful control group, especially
      in analysing the results of the self-report questionnaire;
  (d) a series of in-depth interviews, and visits spanning over two
      years with groups of girls belonging either to the 'Skinheads',
      'Hell's Angels', or 'Greasers'.(5)
   In direct contrast to the previous psychological orientation of
female delinquency studies, the framework adopted in the present
study was to treat delinquency as a social process, in which a
number of social variables could be isolated as influencing the
pattern of female delinquency. This necessitated an examination of
a number of social factors, including sex-role perceptions, social
reactions, group dynamics of delinquent groups, criminal opportunities and so on. However, the areas I would like to concentrate
upon in this paper, because I feel they can ultimately pinpoint the
theoretical direction in which future research may most usefully be
directed, are as follows:
  (a) the nature of female delinquency;
  (b) the influence of social reaction in both confirming everyday
      conceptualisation of female delinquency and also creating a
      possible bias in female criminal statistics;
  (c) the influence of social reaction upon female delinquents
      themselves;
  (d) the group involvement of delinquent girls in what may loosely
      be termed 'delinquent subcultures'.

FINDINGS: THE NATURE OF FEMALE DELINQUENCY

The findings presented in Table 6.1 were the result of a self-report
questionnaire administered to the probation sample, the control
sample and what for convenience I shall hereafter refer to as the
gang sample.
   As far as the restricted nature of female delinquency is concerned, the study supported the fact that sexual misconduct was one
of the offences most frequently committed by both the probation and
gang sample, but notably not the control sample. Attention should
also be drawn to the very small number in the control sample who
admitted to 'running away from home', especially as the analysis of
the court case records showed that this offence resulted in 90 per

TABLE 6.1 Reported delinquent behaviour among girls in three samples

Type of offence	Control sample N = 30 %	Probation sample N = 30 %	Gang sample N = 15 %
Skipped school	63.3	90.0	93.3
Taken articles from a shop	36.7	90.0	80.0
Breaking and entering	10.0	33.3	26.7
Been in a car without the owner's permission	16.7	60.0	60.0
Deliberate property damage	26.7	66.7	73.3
Runaway from home	3.3	70.0	53.3
Had sex relations under age of consent with person of opposite sex	13.3	70.0	73.3
Taken drugs	3.3	10.0	33.3
Taken part in fight	23.3	63.3	73.3

TABLE 6.2   Sentences imposed for survey offences: percentage of offenders receiving sentence for each offence group

Offence group	Conditional discharge %	Fine %	Fit persons order %	Supervision %	Probation %	Approved school %	Percentage of total approved school orders by offence
Care protection and control (N = 35)	-	-	14.3 (5)	54.3 (19)	2.8 (1)	28.6 (10)	58.8
Shoplifting (N = 31)	16.6 (5)	16.1 (5)	3.2 (1)	-	61.4 (19)	3.2 (1)	5.8
Larceny (N = 15)	20.0 (3)	20.0 (3)	-	-	46.7 (7)	13.3 (2)	11.8
Receiving (N = 3)	-	33.3 (1)	-	-	66.7 (2)	-	-
Breaking and entering (N = 3)	-	-	-	-	33.3 (1)	66.7 (2)	11.8
Violence against the person (N = 3)	100 (3)	-	-	-	-	-	-
Take and drive (N = 2)	-	-	-	-	100 (2)	-	-
Malicious damage (N = 2)	-	-	-	-	-	100 (2)	11.8
Breach of probation (N = 1)	-	-	-	-	100 (1)	-	-
Total (N = 95)	11	9	6	19	33	17	100

cent of those referred to court as in need of 'Care, Protection and
Control' attracting the attention of the legal authorities.

In no way, however, does Table 6.1 confirm the hypothesis that
female delinquency was restricted to sexual misconduct. A very high
proportion of both the probation and the gang sample admitted to
deliberate property damage, gang fighting, joy riding, and breaking
and entering. All these offences, as hardly needs stating, are the
very offences that have traditionally been regarded as typical male
crimes, and their under-reporting in female juvenile statistics is
demonstrated by the fact that collectively all four offences accounted for only 8.9 per cent of juvenile offences in Bristol in 1970,
the year in which the self-report questionnaire was administered.
This figure is usefully compared with the 'Care, Protection and
Control' and shoplifting cases which accounted for 69.3 per cent of
all offences in that year.

It is also useful to direct attention to the differences that
exist between delinquent and non-delinquent girls. By using indices
of delinquent behaviour it was possible to specify more precisely
the variety of offences committed by the 'probation' and 'gang'
samples. In fact analysis showed that 80 per cent of the 'gang'
sample and 65 per cent of the 'probation' sample admitted to committing 8 of the 12 delinquent acts listed in the original questionnaire, and this deliberately excluded truancy and sexual misconduct.
When these are included the same proportion admit to committing 10
of the 12 offences. In other words delinquent girls have very often
committed nearly all the offences for which juveniles are usually
referred to court. The equivalent percentage for the control group
was 10 per cent in each case. These findings, besides indicating
that a wider variety of offences are committed by delinquent girls
than has previously been recognised either in official statistics or
by research workers, also confirm earlier findings by Short and Nye
(1958) that there is a certain extremity in female behaviour. Girls
tend to be very conforming or very delinquent.(6)

THE SEXUALISATION OF FEMALE DELINQUENCY

In an attempt to explain this discrepancy between official statistics and the analysis of the self-report study a careful analysis
was made of the 95 court case records. These records (see Table 6.2)
showed quite dramatically that severity of sentence was significantly related to the type of offence committed. Of all the girls
committed to an approved school (now community homes) 58.8 per cent
had been committed for the non-criminal offence of being in need of
'Care, Protection and Control'. Even when social class background
was held constant this relationship was still significant at the
1 per cent level ($x^2 = 26.89$).

Table 6.3 considers the association between family background and
sentence imposed. It shows that approved school orders (i.e., the
most severe sentence under consideration) is eight times more likely
to be given to a girl coming from a broken home than a complete
home. On the other hand fines or conditional discharges (i.e., the
least severe sentence) was in 95 per cent of the court cases examined given to a girl coming from a complete home. This strong

TABLE 6.3   Sentence imposed and family background

Sentence	N	Family complete (% receiving sentence)	Family broken (% receiving sentence)
Probation	33	54.5	45.5
Supervision	19	36.8	63.2
Approved school	17	11.8	88.2
Fine and conditional discharge	20	95.0	5.0
Fit persons order	6	50.0	50.0

association between home background and severity of sentence was found to be significant at the 1 per cent level in the case of both approved school orders and fines and conditional discharges.

However, before reaching any definitive conclusions concerning the selectivity of judicial action, the findings presented in Table 6.4 must be carefully borne in mind. This table shows as one may expect, that those classified as being in need of 'Care, Protection and Control' show the highest incidences of broken homes. Therefore, the relationship between approved school orders and 'Care, Protection and Control' cases, which has already been demonstrated (see Table 6.2) becomes somewhat problematic; as it is unclear whether it is the existence of a broken home, or type of offence committed, or both, that is the main concern of the law enforcement agencies when passing sentence.

TABLE 6.4   Offence group and family background

Offence group	N	Family broken (% in specific offence category)	Family complete (% in specific offence category)
'Care, Protection and Control'	35	62.85	37.14
Shoplifting	31	38.7	61.3
Larceny	15	40.0	60.0
Other	14	42.9	57.1

Unfortunately the numbers involved here are too small to separate the variables of broken homes and offence category. All one can say with any degree of certainty is that a statistically significant selectivity by judicial authorities takes place, in that they are more likely to send a girl to an approved school if she comes from a broken home or has been referred to court as in need of 'Care, Protection and Control'. It is quite impossible however, to say which of these two variables is the more important.

A possible interpretation of the data is that the variable of broken homes is an extension of the 'Care, Protection and Control' complex. The existence of a broken home acts so as to heighten the chances that a parent will make an official complaint to one of the law enforcing agencies. It seems, after all, not unreasonable to suppose that where a mother (or father) is alone faced with the problem of a 'defiant' or 'delinquent' daughter she is likely not only to seek the aid of official agencies, but when matters really come to a head, as is the case once her daughter is 'picked up' by the police as having 'run away from home', she may then be more easily tempted or provoked into asserting that she can no longer control her daughter. Whilst, in the 'complete' family there is likely to be not only more internal familial support to cope with the girl's problematic behaviour, but perhaps also a stronger concern with external respectability which means that parents will attempt to 'protect' their daughter from any official action which may follow from too many serious complaints.

If this is correct, the relationship between broken homes and 'Care, Protection and Control' cases may indeed by a spurious one created by parental decision on the one hand, and the selectivity and expectations of the law enforcing agencies on the other. But in any case the relationship between female delinquency, sexual delinquency and broken homes begins to appear more and more as a statistical artifact which the predominant concern with a 'double standard of morality' has partially created and perpetuated. The data so far discussed illustrate that girls in approved schools have been administratively selected on two accounts. First, they are more likely to have been incarcerated if referred to court as in need of 'Care, Protection and Control' - hence the assumed relationship between female delinquency and sexual delinquency; second, they are the most likely 'delinquent group' to have come from broken homes, hence the prominence of the further assumption concerning the relationship between female delinquents and abnormal and pathological characteristics.

Although my own research made no direct comparisons with males, two studies in America (Chesney-Lind, 1973; Terry, 1970) have taken further this issue of the sexualisation of criminal offences. In the study by Terry (1970) it was shown that girls suspected of sexual offences and incorrigibility were far more likely to have charges brought against them than males. This finding is supported by the fact that self-support studies (Gold, 1970; Wise, 1967) have shown sexual offences, incorrigibility and running away from home to be more frequently committed by males than females. These offences in America in 1964 accounted for 74.5 per cent of female delinquent referrals but only 27.5 per cent of the male referrals. Furthermore, Chesney-Lind (1973) found that proportionately three times as many females as males were institutionalised for committing this offence, lending no support at all to the thesis that females are more leniently treated. There is little reason to suppose that the situation is different in the United Kingdom. Besides the selectivity demonstrated in my own findings, Richardson (1969) suggested that there is every reason to suppose that offences by girls are sexualised, in fact non-sexual offences are overlooked in favour of sexual (mis)-behaviour. My own interviews fully support this, comments like the following being quite common:

Kathy: 'It's funny because once when I was down the cop shop for
fighting, this woman saw the swastika on my arm and forgot all
about what she was looking for. They never did nothing - just
told me to stop fighting. But the woman cop, she kept on about
the swastika and Hell's Angels. What a bad lot they were for a
girl to go around with, and how I had better stop going around
with the Angels or else I'd get a really bad name for myself.
Then she kept asking me if I'd had sex with any of 'em or taken
drugs.'

Kathy was only brought to court when her father complained to the
Children's Department that she was beyond his control and stayed out
most nights.

This process results, of course, in official statistics showing
a high rate of sexual delinquency for girls and consequent severe
punishment for many female offenders. It is only when the practices
of the juvenile magistrates' courts are examined that it is revealed
that a sexual bias in court proceedings actually influences the
picture of female juvenile delinquency presented in the official
statistics.

EFFECTS OF THE SEXUALISATION OF JUVENILE OFFENCES

So far attention has been focused upon the process of sexualisation
by judicial agencies. I would like now to draw more specific attention to the way delinquent girls themselves perceived the condemning
remarks made about them by parents, teachers and non-delinquent
associates. The strong awareness of disapproval is indicated in the
following accounts:

Anne: 'I've been told loads of times that it's not feminine, it's
unnatural to fight. You look so common and cheap when you fight.
    Our mum says to me why can't I be like other girls and tells
me that it's horrible to see girls fighting. So I say to her, "I
suppose you would rather me come home beat up than not to fight?"
And then she says, "Oh no." I don't think she knows what she
wants really.'

Sandra: 'We get drunk every Friday and Saturday we do. And the
boys and other girls give us the most filthiest of looks. We
arrange to meet someone and of course you get pissed and go off
with somebody else, and they say, "Oh, isn't she cheap", and
that, just because you're drunk.'

Liz: 'Look I don't believe there should be one standard for a
boy and another for a girl. But there just is round here and
there's not much you can do about it. A chap's going to look for
someone who hasn't had it off with every bloke. So as soon as
you let them put a leg over you, you've got a bad name.'

Linda: 'Sometimes at school, like you get mad and go and smash
something up. Like this one day I grabbed hold of this thing and
smashed it through the toilet window. Well, I did do wrong but

you should have heard our headmistress. She said I was a common looking slut, and the most vulgar common girl she had known.'

The existence of some kind of double standard of morality was accepted by most of the girls. The continual reference to them as sluts and common prostitutes did not, however, seem to have the effect that Reiss (1960) suggests of involving girls in a vicious circle of status loss, promiscuity, further status loss, aggravated promiscuity and so forth. In fact most of the girls interviewed tended to react, if anything, with aggressive rather than promiscuous behaviour. Also, contrary to previous empirical evidence (Morris, 1964), they seemed popular amongst their peers.

However, the severe attitude to adult authorities in their sexual labelling of the girls did suggest that many of them suffered from what I have referred to elsewhere (Shacklady, 1972) as a 'double rejection'. They were rejected first on account of the fact that they had violated legal norms and second because in contrast to males, whose delinquent behaviour is often seen as an *extension* of their role, they were seen to have offended against their own sex-role, and the traditional stereotyped conceptions of femininity.

The importance of recognising this 'double rejection' is that it enables attention to be focused more directly upon the moral judgments applied to female delinquent behaviour, rather than upon the delinquents themselves, the focus of most previous research. Undoubtedly the judgments most frequently applied were those of being 'sluttish', 'prostitutes' and 'common'. Evidence from the interviews suggested that these labels had not been accepted - there seemed to be a particular resistance on the part of the girls to seeing themselves as promiscuous, a form of behaviour strongly condemned by most of the girls in the study. What they did develop were self-conceptions as tough, dominant and tomboyish.

It may well be that a further consequence of the double standard of morality is that it effectively isolates delinquent girls from most of their non-delinquent peers. Time and again girls complained that they were not allowed to mix with a particular girl, because their mothers would let them have nothing to do with girls who had been in trouble with legal authorities. Though the same isolation has been found in male studies (Dinits et al., 1960) most of the girls were quite emphatic in stating that nothing like the same controls were exerted over their brothers, a finding, of course, well supported in the literature on sex-differences (Nye, 1959). This form of social ostracism quite naturally was counteracted by greater dependency upon delinquent groups, where the female's participation, far from being passive, involved a heavy emphasis on fighting, shoplifting and drinking. It may well be therefore that as Matza (1964) and others have suggested, the attribution of delinquent definitions to males leads to exaggerated patterns of masculine behaviour, while in the case of females, it leads to reactive unfeminine behaviour. If this is the case then social definitions of female delinquency lead not so much to a total rejection of femininity in that a male role is aspired to, as to a rejection of certain elements of a culturally stereotyped female role which is perceived by the girls as too constraining.

If this interpretation is correct it would also seem to account

for the greater extremities in female delinquent behaviour. Where
criminal labels are applied to females they are so pervasive that
they are more or less bound to force girls into more extreme forms
of delinquency. For though a more protective attitude appears to be
taken by probation officers, social workers and others, the paradox
of this protection is that it leads to more severe labelling of
their behaviour as being 'common' and 'sluttish'. Thus, long before
they had reached the courts, all the girls interviewed had experienced a continual defining process which classified them as unfeminine.

In view of these facts it is my firm belief that a labelling
approach far from being irrelevant to female delinquency studies is
absolutely necessary in understanding their pattern of delinquent
activities.

GROUP MEMBERSHIP OF DELINQUENT GIRLS

Reference has been made in this paper to 'delinquent groups'. The
definitional difficulties involved in using such a term are fully
recognised, but used within this context it is meant to imply no
more than that a high proportion of delinquent girls (89.6 per cent)
belonged to a group whose central requirement seems to be that of
committing delinquent acts (Cloward and Ohlin, 1961).

The complete absence of subcultural theories within studies of
female delinquency has already been alluded to. The reasons given
for this neglect range from the assumption that girls never form
gangs, to the belief that as female membership of a gang is only
through a boyfriend, analysts should focus on the male/female
dyadic relationship rather than the girls' own group involvement.

As far as the first assumption is concerned, the present study
found no direct evidence of a female delinquent subculture as such.
Rather, the girls were members of male-dominated groups like Skinheads, Greasers and Hell's Angels. What concerned me most, however,
was the girl's position within these groups. In contrast to the
descriptions (7) presented by Downes (1966) and Flyvel (1963) where
girls were seen as peripheral to the main activities of male dominated groups, the girls interviewed in my study left me in no doubt
of the fact that their group involvement was serious. Moreover,
their active participation was illustrated by some of the following
comments:

Skinhead: 'Well since I was about 14 I was a member of the Skinheads and I liked the sort of bother Skinheads made and I liked
all the news they got, nice to see people taking notice of us at
last. Mind you we've got a bad name with everyone round here.
The Bristol Skinheads are really hard and the cops hate us. But,
you know, we're just a gang of friends really. If anyone hit
anyone of us there would be war. I mean you've just got to
stick up for your mates. You've got to be a good fighter or
you're not really one of the gang.'

Skinhead: 'They treat us really well. I mean, they don't
exploit us or nothing. They treat us as equal. We all get

together and make all the big decisions and we all go to the big
fights. I think they respect us, and that, more now because if
we're going anywhere they know we'll support them. I think that's
very good because when we were down in Weston the girls there
wouldn't do nothing. They had "Hell's Angels Weston" and all the
colours on their back. Colours are meant to be so important to
the Angels. Yet I went up like to one girl and I ripped her
colours off and she just said "Sorry, don't do that - that's my
jacket". With that she really made me aggro. I went mad like
because in Bristol anyone will have a fight with you, and if you
ripped an Angels colours off she'd really go wild. All the
Bristol Angels would, you would be knifed and there would be no
more to do about it. But what really got me was that they
wouldn't stand up for their mates. If they were in Bath we'd
soon make it obvious we didn't want them. Because I mean that's
why I always carry a knife or razor. You've always got to try
and stick by your mates.'

Hell's Angel: 'I know people think we sleep around and that,
but that's not how most of us feel. If you're going steady with
a bloke it's all right. But going from one boy to another it's
not really right, because you usually find there's a lot of
trouble through that. You know one girl goes off with another
girl's chap and somebody gets jealous. This can cause trouble
within the group. I think it's alright if you're not a member
of the group, but no one likes it within our group.'

Skinhead: 'I reckon we fight as seriously as the boys. You
know, if anybody comes up to us we'll smack a bottle in their
faces. You know we say, "you try it", and they don't think we
will use it on them. But we will if they try anything. The real
trouble comes though when we go down the "Porch" and "Christopher".
That's like our territory. Any Greasers or Hairies come in and
there's trouble. We'll leave each other alone inside but as
soon as we're outside we'll really start fighting. I always
carry a knife or bog chain when I go down there.'

These accounts not only demonstrate the extensive nature of the
girls' delinquent behaviour, but also throw considerable doubt on
the assertions of earlier gang researchers. Clearly, things seem to
have changed since the days of Downes (1966) and Flyvel (1963) both
of whom partially substantiate their claims that subcultural
theories are inappropriate for the study of female delinquency, by
reference to their findings that girls' membership in groups tends
to be of much shorter duration than that of males. My own findings
confirm that girls are indeed members for a shorter period of time
- being members on average for 2½ years in comparison with the
males' 4 years. However, the reasons for leaving were in no way
dependent on termination of relationships with individual boyfriends. Generally they were forced to leave by early pregnancy
and the marriage that this usually precipitated.
My purpose in presenting this brief account of the girls involvement in delinquent groups has been to draw attention to the fact
that because of preconceptions concerning the girls' lack of need,

or even ability, to join various groups there has been an unwarran-
ted neglect of the dynamics of delinquent girls' group relationships.
The full extent of the girls' commitment and its effects upon their
self-concept, and social reaction from a variety of authorities
including parents, teachers and social workers have not been fully
explored. However, the importance of group membership has been
demonstrated here and future research could usefully examine more
fully some of these variables.

CONCLUSION

The data presented seems to disprove the four hypotheses which
have underlined much of the previous research in this area.
Although more evidence is needed to prove conclusively that official
agencies sexualise offences, the evidence certainly suggests that it
is not possible to accept official statistics as unproblematic and
thereby equate female delinquency with sexual delinquency. Similarly there is every reason to believe that subcultural theory can
contribute to our understanding of female delinquency.
    There can in view of these findings be little doubt that more
critical sociological research is now needed in the much neglected
area of female criminality. Although the prime concern of this
paper has been to empirically demonstrate the fact that 'common-
sense' assumptions about female delinquency are on closer examination fallacious, I was also concerned to emphasise the relationship
between female delinquency and social reaction. A cognisance of
such reaction is important for three reasons - first, it explains
why official statistics are biased in the way they are, second, it
is one of the most important elements in the processual development
of secondary delinquent behaviour patterns, and third, since it
encourages an active reliance upon delinquent groups, the point is
emphasised that the girls' behaviour cannot be understood without
an examination of the social dynamics of such groups.
    In conclusion, I would like to stress that deviant definitions
are never static. I have emphasised in this paper the sexualising
of offences, and the consequent sexual label applied to delinquent
girls. Since deviant definitions are inevitably related to the
social position of the group concerned, it follows that any real or
perceived change in the economic and political position of women
may well lead to a redefinition of female criminality by judicial
authorities and the media. It could well be argued that the
recent increase in officially recorded violence among girls indicates that a change in definition, rather than behaviour per se has
already taken place. Such a change may ultimately lead to a conceptualisation of the female delinquent as more of a threat to 'law
and order' and not just, as at present, as a threat to the maintenance of sexual mores.

NOTES

1 Expressions of concern and attendant explanations still contain
many sexist assumptions. Either the increase is exaggerated out
of all proportion and blamed on the Women's Movement rather than
seeing both as the outcome of changing social and economic conditions, or, as in the case of the now notorious political
offenders - Anna Mendelson, Hilary Creek, Leila Khaled and the
Price Sisters - editorials lay great stress on attempting to
explain why 'nice middle-class girls' could possibly turn into
violent anarchists.

2 This is not to deny that there are differences associated with
differential illegitimate and legitimate opportunity. But it
is of crucial importance not to get so obsessed with these
differences that assumptions concerning the causation are never
explicitly stated. Indeed, the literature is filled with statements like 'common sense suggests that the main factors are
somatic ones, especially hormonal ones ...' (Cowie et al., 1968).

3 This acceptance has had the unfortunate consequence of directing
theorists to a prime concern with female criminality *in relation*
to male criminality and thereby not to female criminality as a
subject worthy of study in its own right.

4 It should be pointed out that this sample was selected by the
probation officers concerned, who were reluctant to have certain
cases jeopardised by a research worker. However, the numbers
were so small the 30 interviewees were in fact drawn from a
total sample of 38.

5 This was a self-selected group. All the girls interviewed were
volunteers whom I got to know before the study began, or was put
directly in contact with whilst carrying out the fieldwork. For
a more detailed account of the methods used see Shacklady (1972).

6 This is in direct contrast to most other observed sex-differences
where females deviate less than males from the mean.

7 Clearly, it is possible that things have changed since the days
of Downes (1966) and Flyvel (1963). Perhaps girls used to be
more peripheral and have recently become more central in gangs.

7 Accounting for rape
Reality and myth in press reporting

Carol Smart and Barry Smart

The incidence of rape in Britain now appears to be increasing
although it has not yet achieved the status of a pressing social
problem as it has in the USA where it has been referred to as the
'all American crime' (Griffin, 1971). Between 1969 and 1975 there
has been an increase of 20 per cent in the number of rapes known to
the police in England and Wales. Unfortunately, as is the case
with crime statistics in general, there is no way of achieving a
precise knowledge of the percentage increase in actual rapes, there
being an immeasurable disparity between the real incidence of rape
and the number of rapes actually reported to the police or leading
to a conviction in court. In addition to this there is the considerable problem of the current legal definition of rape and its
adequacy, both in theory and in practice, for differentiating
between rape and non-rape in the legal process. The difficulty of
legally proving that a rape has occurred is now quite well documented elsewhere (Coote and Gill, 1975; Smart, 1976) but essentially
it means that even when a rape charge reaches court the chances
against securing a conviction are very high because of the technical
requirements affecting the evidence presented in court. Rape is
therefore not only under-reported at the police level but under-
represented in conviction rate statistics.

It is not unreasonable to assume, however, that the increase in
known rapes has been accompanied by an increase in undisclosed or
unreported rapes, although the ratio of known or reported rapes to
unreported rapes, and possible changes in this ratio, are at
present a matter of speculation. Certainly in the American context
there seems to have been an increase in both reported rapes and
unreported rapes and in Britain the increasing attention devoted to
the law on rape has itself produced an awareness of the extent of
undisclosed rapes which previously had been considered insignificant.
However, given the nature of the offence it is certain that the real
figure will remain 'hidden', the very dimensions, contexts and forms
of rape, rape in marriage, by a 'friend' or 'acquaintance' or
neighbour, by an employer etc. create circumstances which are likely,
other things being equal, to ensure that a significant proportion of
rapes will remain unreported to the police. Indeed the law, criminal
process, police activity and attitudes towards victims themselves go

a long way towards implicitly or explicitly discouraging women from reporting sexual assaults or taking their assailants to court (Smart, 1976).

There has for some time now been a growth of public interest in, and expression of concern over, the increasing incidence of rape. Manifestations of this growing concern are evident in first, an increase in the attention generally devoted by the press to the phenomenon of rape, for example reports on the cases of specific women who have been raped, e.g. Joan Little and Inez Garcia in America,(1) discussion of the controversy aroused by specific judgments in rape cases in Britain, e.g., the cases involving Judge Christmas Humphreys and Judge Edward Sutcliffe,(2) and analyses of the operation of the law on rape and Parliamentary discussion of possible legislative changes. Second, a recognition of the importance of rape crisis centres for the support of the victims of rape. Third, an increase in feminist analysis, writing and action on the problem of rape in the USA and, to a much lesser extent, in the UK (Brownmiller, 1975; Connell and Wilson, 1974). Finally, legislative activity to modify the law on rape, in particular to make the court-room procedure for the victim of rape less traumatic by modifying the rules of evidence, as well as to clarify the question of consent in the legal conception of rape.

Since the infamous D.P.P. v. Morgan and others case in 1975 and the subsequent Law Lords' ruling on rape which aroused concern over the question of consent in rape cases, rape has been a crime which has aroused a considerable amount of interest in the press and has provoked much public discussion. Since the case of D.P.P. v. Morgan is well documented elsewhere (cf. All England Law Reports, 1976; Coote and Gill, 1975), it will suffice here to note that the basic issue in the case concerned the question of the intention (mens rea) to commit rape. The case eventually went to the House of Lords on appeal and in a majority decision the Law Lords ruled that a man could be acquitted of the charge of rape even where his belief that the victim consented to sexual intercourse was unreasonable. Although this decision did not alter the outcome of the Morgan case, other imprisoned rapists were able to win their release on the grounds that the 'reasonableness' of their belief in their victim's consent was a critical and ultimately condemning factor in their trials and therefore lead to their convictions.(3) Moreover the fear was expressed that any men accused of rape would be able to use the Law Lords' decision to win an acquittal, thus creating a situation in which men could commit rape almost at will, the Law Lords' decision being seen as a 'rapist's charter'.

Following this series of events in 1975 the Government set up an Advisory Group on the Law of Rape which published its recommendations for reform in December 1975. This was immediately followed by a Private Member's Bill, the Sexual Offences (Amendment) Bill, which became law in December 1976 (cf. Smart, 1976).

Although during this period of time there was a general increase in press coverage of rape, in particular concerning the passage of legislation, discussion of specific cases and legal issues (e.g., the question of consent), the stock-in-trade press coverage continued to be the novelette style account of a rape case, involving specific details of participants, the situation and sequence of

events. In such reports no attempt is made to situate the specific
selected incident within its determining socio-cultural context
which alone would make possible an understanding of the phenomenon
of rape, the social conditions which make such sexual assaults
possible, and the socio-historical and material processes which
have produced both the present form of sexual relations and the
understanding or consciousness of these existing relations as
'naturally' based. We will argue that the increase in press attention to rape has not improved understanding of the nature of
forceful sexual assaults on women. On the contrary the general
form and content of rape reporting have served to further confound
a rational understanding of rape as well as to indirectly conspire
to perpetuate women's social and sexual subordination by producing
rape reports which serve as both a form of sexual titillation and
as a veiled 'warning' to non-conforming 'independent' women, that
is to say as an implicit form of social control.

CULTURAL ASSUMPTIONS ABOUT RAPE

Rape is legally defined as unlawful sexual intercourse by a man
with a woman (who is not his legal wife) without her consent, by
means of force, threat or fraud. This apparently unproblematic
definition has, however, proved to be manifestly inadequate in
practice. In the first instance it excludes the rape of a woman
by her husband, the rape law stating that wives have no legal
right to refuse to have sexual intercourse with their marriage
partners. Second, it excludes forms of sexual humiliation such as
penetration with inanimate objects or forced oral sex. Third, the
issue of consent by the victim, which is vital in most cases of
rape, is highly controversial; this is a consequence of the com-
plexity of human sexuality, the considerable, at times extreme,
differences in moral codes and sexual attitudes, the existence of
double standards of behaviour for men and women, as well as conflicting expectations, and both 'legitimate' and illegitimate forms of
sexual exploitation (i.e., rape inside and outside marriage). In
consequence it may be extremely difficult for a raped woman to
convince others (police, doctors, relatives) that she has indeed
been raped. Moreover, prevailing conceptions of rape present in
'common-sense' understandings, in press reports and within the
criminal process, exemplify specific stereotypes of male-female
sexual relations, male and female sexuality, and in particular rely
upon specific myths about female sexuality.
    Perhaps the most significant prevailing cultural stereotype of
rape is that involving a brutal assault where the aggressor is a
sexual psychopath unable to contain or control his desires and the
victim is the woman innocent, naive or 'foolish' enough to leave
herself vulnerable to attack by being in an isolated space
(socially or geographically), usually after dark or 'curfew'. This
stereotype has been much used by generations of parents who have
prudently, given the existing social circumstances, warned their
young daughters of the perils that lurk beyond the domestic threshold of conformity. Such imagery has also been widely employed in
films and literature and by the police in the cause of crime

prevention (Crime Prevention Department, 1976).(4)

However, as is frequently the case with stereotypes, the stereotype of rape is far removed from the reality. It has been revealed
that rape in fact occurs in more commonplace situations than is
conventionally believed (and reported) to be the case. Amir (1967),
for example, in his study of 646 known rapes in Philadelphia
between 1958 and 1960, shows that 48.9 per cent of the victims and
offenders in rape cases were 'known' to each other. By 'known'
Amir means acquaintances, neighbours, friends, and family friends
and relatives. Only just over a half of the total number of cases
studied involved total strangers. Moreover Amir's evidence indicates that it is not in woods, on isolated moorlands or in dark
alleys that rape is most likely to occur but actually in the home
of either the victim or the offender. In fact 55.7 per cent of
rapes took place in the home, 14.9 per cent in a car and 29.4 per
cent elsewhere. Although the street was the most common place for
initial contact between rapist and victim (48.5 per cent of cases),
the victim's home was the next most common (26.5 per cent). It
would seem therefore from this study that the domestic realm contains as many dangers of rape for women as do more public and
impersonal places, and that women are in as much danger from
acquaintances and friends as from strangers.

Equally significant data from Amir's (1971) study shows that a
large percentage of rapes are planned rather than spontaneous
responses to sexual arousal or opportunity. He found that 70 per
cent of the rapes listed in police files were planned; that is the
place of the rape was pre-arranged, the victim was deliberately
sought out and plans were made for enticement or coercion, only
15.9 per cent of the rapes were 'explosive' or totally unplanned.
In consequence Amir's evidence on the extent of planned rape
indicates that individual victims are less responsible for the
attacks from which they suffer than is usually assumed to be the
case. The danger or threat of rape resides more in the fact that
women in general are the objects of male sexual or aggressive
feelings than in the fact that particular women make themselves
vulnerable or encourage attack. Indeed a large number of victims
of rape are women who fall outside the customary category of being
sexually attractive or alluring. Women in their 60s and 70s are
not immune from rape, neither for that matter are girls under 10
years of age, nor are heavily pregnant women or so-called 'plain'
women.

Studies of known male rapists (cf. Amir, 1971; Gilley, 1974)
further serve to challenge the prevailing cultural stereotype of
rape. Most rapists are not sexual psychopaths nor are they insane.
Amir (1971) has shown that among men convicted of rape there is no
strong indication of sexual abnormality, in fact these men differed
from 'normal' males (presumably non-rapists) only in having a
greater tendency to express violence and rage. Moreover the sentencing policy of the courts in both the UK and USA does not support
the view that rapists are psychopathic or even dangerous offenders.
Although in the UK a conviction for rape may result in a life
sentence, it rarely does. The most common prison sentence for rape
in the UK is now 2 to 3 years (cf. Smart, 1976) and although imprisonment is the most usual punishment, offenders in some cases receive

fines, probation and suspended sentences. Relatively few convicted rapists are dealt with under the Mental Health Act of 1959 and of those who are sent to prison, again very few receive psychiatric treatment (Gilley, 1974). Our legal and penal systems therefore do not treat most rapists any differently from other offenders and those rapists who are defined as mentally ill represent only a small minority.

Significantly the sexual motivation for rape is now being called into question. Rather than an outcome or 'release' of sexual desire, as is so commonly assumed to be the case, rape is seen to be an act of violence and domination in which sexual activity becomes the means to totally debase and dehumanise the victim. Alternatively rape may serve as a means for symbolically proving manhood to other males, this is especially the case where gang rapes occur, or even in certain circumstances, for example in the case of impotence, for the rapist himself. Sexual gratification alone is not, therefore, the basis of rape, on the contrary such an assault is the means to achieve other ulterior ends which may be unrelated to, or independent of, the specific rape victim, her behaviour or her social or physical characteristics.

The rape stereotype is consequently unlikely to fit many rape victim's actual experiences, although in certain cases it may (e.g., in the case of the Cambridge Rapist).(5) In those cases where there is a lack of congruence between cultural expectations or understandings of rape and the rape itself, there may well follow a reticence on the part of the victim to define the assault as rape, doubts may intrude into the victim's understanding of her ordeal as to whether she unconsciously or unknowingly 'encouraged' or precipitated the assault. Thus the rape victim may begin to engage in a process of self-criticism and blame, itself a corollary of a widely held view of rape, namely that 'the victim wants to be humiliated otherwise she cannot be taken' (cf. Gratus, 1976). Frequently such cases, namely those where there is a lack of con-gruence between the cultural stereotype and the particular assault, are treated as bogus, the victim considered to have in fact 'agreed' to sexual intercourse and then to have 'cried rape' after the event out of spite, fear, or some other motive. Furthermore, even where an 'atypical' or 'non-stereotypical' rape has been proven, the victim of the assault may not be vindicated, she may in fact be held responsible in some part for the assault.(6)

ACCOUNTS OF RAPE

Descriptions or accounts of rape and rape imagery appear in various media forms, in film, on television, in advertising, and in the press, as well as within the literary and novel form. In many cases the accounts of rape which appear are in fact imaginary constructions presented within a dramatic form rather than attempts at explaining rape or describing actual rapes. Now there are important differences between news reports and fictional or imag-inary accounts. In particular in terms of the referent, for example an event occurring in the real world in contrast to an imaginary construction for a film or television drama, and also in

terms of intention, for example attempting to offer an accurate
report of an event rather than to stimulate a dramatic response in
an audience or reader, or to develop the identity of a particular
character as in the novel form. However we will attempt to show
that there are significant underlying similarities in both forms
of rape account.

Before proceeding to consider specific accounts of rape, and
press reports in particular, it is important to recognise that the
topic should be located within the general context of media images
of women, and within the context of news reporting. For example,
it has been argued that conventional journalistic practices produce texts which first render women 'invisible' by employing the
masculine term as generic and inclusive of the feminine, or
second describe women in terms of specific character, occupational,
and social stereotypes, thereby reinforcing the prevailing repressive conception of women's lives, interests, ambitions and abil-
ities, neglecting completely the significance for many women of
work outside the home, or of political and trade-union activity.
(Equality Working Party of the National Union of Journalists, 1975,
p.4). We can observe that within the press there exists a differential distribution of images of women ranging from the 'Sun's'
daily glamour girl pin-up through to the wife, mother and career
woman, and that these images are located within specific texts,
reports or photographs on a variety of topics from news reports to
advertisements, feature articles and cartoons. The cumulative
significance of press representations of women or events involving
women is itself a neglected area, as indeed is the question of the
range of possible interpretations or meanings made available to a
reader of a specific report, on for example a sexual assault,
which itself is situated alongside, below or above a variety of
other texts which treat women as sex-objects (intrinsic), as
objects of humour, or as sex-objects (instrumental) for promoting
a specific commodity, as in advertising.

A commonly voiced criticism of newspaper reporting is that news
is all too often separated from news analysis, that is to say,
issues are presented in abstraction from the contexts within which
they need to be situated in order that an adequate understanding
may follow (cf. Birt and Jay, 1975). One possible consequence of
conventional news procedure is therefore that news reports reduce
the issue or topic with which they are concerned to an event
involving specific characters or personalities alone and thereby
fail to address the socio-economic, historical, and cultural
context of which the event is a realisation. Such news reports,
rather than generating understanding, or correcting misunderstand-
ings of an event by situating the phenomenon within its socio-
cultural context, tend to dwell upon the specific idiosyncratic
characteristics of the particular event, trade off and indeed
ultimately perpetuate commonly held conceptions or stereotypes of
the phenomenon. Thus is made possible the innocent consumption of
myth as fact. This is nowhere more true than in the case of rape
reporting.

As we have noted the media produce both fictional accounts or
imaginary reconstructions, and news reports or realist accounts of
rape situations. Rape scenes appear in literature, novels and

magazines, and increasingly on film. Now although such rape
accounts need to be distinguished from press reports of rape, in
so far as the latter are, however problematically, related to real
events, whereas the former are ostensibly imaginary constructions,
the central themes in literary and film explanations or accounts
of rape and descriptions of the characters involved in rape
scenarios closely resemble the comparable structures present
in press reports or accounts of rape. This will become clearer
through a brief examination of the central characteristics of novel
and film representations of rape. Characteristically rape is
depicted in one of the following three ways, as:
(a) The epitome of male-female sexual relationships.
(b) An exceptional, pathological event; an isolated rather than
    socially structured crime.
(c) A victim-precipitated assault, the woman being responsible for
    her own fate.
   Rarely in fictional accounts of rape is there any reference to
the socio-cultural structuring of male-female sexual relations,
rather rape is portrayed as an inevitable consequence of existing
relationships between men and women. As such, a rape scene in a
novel tends to endorse the specific violent and forced experience
as the epitome of sexual encounters rather than as a criminal act.
Consider for example the account of Luke's rape of Arlene in
Rhinehart's 'The Dice Man' (1972). At no stage in the account of
the sequence of events is any consideration given to the rape as a
crime, rather Luke's expression of his intention to commit rape,
his advances and violence towards Arlene and the report of their
conversation serve to perpetuate the view that women are unconsciously wanting to be 'taken'. Arlene having been told of Luke's
intention, 'I've come downstairs to rape you', and after having
been beaten around the face, eventually submits to his demands.
      'I want to rape you Arlene. Now, this moment. Let's go'.
      'All right', she said and with a look which I can only
   describe as righteous indignation, began to move past me down
   the hall towards the bedroom, adding, 'But you leave Jake's
   [the husband's] bathrobe alone.' (Rhinehart, 1972, p.56)
We are then told that the rape was consummated and that the
pleasure was primarily Arlene's. Indeed the only expression of
concern that Arlene is allowed in the context of the rape is for
Jake, her husband, namely that *he* 'won't like it'. In Rhinehart's
description rape is presented as the very epitome of male-female
sexual relations.
   Conversely rape may be depicted as merely an exceptional or
freak event, as something that happens to *other* women in *abnormal*
circumstances. In such instances the relationship between a
culture that exploits women and the phenomenon of rape is again
left entirely undisclosed. In the words of one feminist writer,
rape is considered only as a 'hateful isolated crime with no social
underpinnings' (Farrow, 1974, p.99). A variation on this theme
occurs where authors offer accounts of rape as an exceptional,
pathological event by dwelling upon the specific idiosyncrasies of
the rapist, in particular structuring a motive for the crime in
terms of sexual deprivation or frustration.
   The third way in which rape may be depicted is as a form of

victim-precipitated assault. Basically there are two versions of
this 'thesis', one an explicit version in which men are portrayed
as the victims of situations over which they have no control,
situations which are set up or constructed by independent women
(cf. Farrow, 1974),(7) the other an implicit version in which the
woman is made to experience further punishment and suffering as a
consequence of being the victim of a rape. On the latter version
Farrow notes that the rape victim is frequently portrayed in literature and films as experiencing further retribution, that is to
say being forced to have the baby, becoming a lesbian, turning to
prostitution, or committing suicide. She observes that these
outcomes, which assume a material form in the novel or film, are
a representation of the 'cultural belief that the rape victim
should be punished', that the raped woman must have asked for it,
rather than an imaginary reconstruction of the actual consequences
of rape for rape victims. Now although we may agree with the view
that the specific outcomes referred to above 'almost never happen
in real life to rape victims', that the rape victim does not now
have to have a baby, that lesbianism does not follow as a consequence, and in any case cannot with any credibility be considered a punishment, it does seem to be the case that rape victims
may suffer further, as a consequence of being raped, in so far as
they are often treated badly by doctors, the police, their husbands,
friends and neighbours. In other words it is not just the cultural
belief that the rape victim should be punished which finds its way
into the story, rather the consequence of rape for the victim as
portrayed in novels and films represents a dramatic translation of
the material reality of rape and the social practices that follow
as a consequence.

We will show that the very same cultural values and forms of
representation of rape that are characteristic of novel and film
accounts of rape permeate and structure press reports of rape.

PRESS REPORTS

One of the most evident characteristics of press reports of rape is
that the specific rape reported in the newspaper is a 'selected'
rape, that is to say it is merely one illustration or example of
the general phenomenon and can not be considered as representative.
Brownmiller (1975), within the context of her general discussion of
rape, makes a few observations on this topic. She notes that
although New York City police statistics indicated that white
women were less often victims of rape than black women, and
furthermore that victims ranged in age from seventy-four years to
pre-teens, that the most common rape story covered by the 'New York
Daily News' was of the atypical young, white, middle-class 'attractive' victim.

Clearly rape reporting may vary from one paper to another, from
a straight report in the so-called 'quality' press of an offence
having been committed or a judgment having been reached to a lurid,
titillating or vicarious report in a 'tabloid' newspaper. It is
the latter kind of report of which Brownmiller writes, noting that
the rape story in such papers in frequently 'enhanced by certain

elements of glamour ... is ... dressed up to fit the male fantasy'
(1975, p.337). Her explanation of this form of rape reporting,
namely that tabloid editors assume sex sells papers and that for
men editing for a primarily male readership sex means woman, is not
however confined in relevance to the American press alone. What
emerges from Brownmiller's brief account is that the rape story has
a dual status for the tabloid paper, it is at one and the same time
a news or crime story and a sex-feature. This is clearly also the
case in respect of the 'sensational' or tabloid press in Britain,
in particular the 'Sun's' and the 'News of the World's' reporting
of rape cases. Indeed, the latter's reputation is itself probably
dependent upon the column inches it devotes to the presentation of
novelette style accounts of specific sex crimes.

At present there are few analyses of British press reports of
rape. In consequence information is limited to a few observations
concerning specific characteristics of the content. For example it
has been noted that only a small proportion of rape assaults get
any sustained coverage (e.g., two or more reports in the same
newspaper), that, just as in the case of the American press, it
would appear from press reports that only 'attractive' women get
raped, and that press reports of rape have generally kept pace with
the increase in rape as reported in the criminal statistics. In
our analysis of the text of rape reports we are interested in the
presentation of the victim, the description of the rapist, the
explanation of the incident, and attribution of motive and responsibility for the assault. It is our view that the rape report must
be considered as a text situated first, within and alongside other
texts, both literal and photographic, within the specific newspaper
concerned, as well as second, embedded within and drawing upon a
system of cultural values that both assist and inform the writing
of the report and in addition make available a specific interpretation or reading of the report. As the context within which rape
reports are located is likely to be indicative of the status of
such reports (for example as sex rather than crime news) for both
newspaper editors and readership we must consider cautiously the
significance of reports of rape which lie within the same overall
newspaper text as 'pin-up' photographs, advertisements featuring
women as sexual objects, and cartoons depicting women as sexual
objects. Furthermore, the literary style of reporting for example
the 'News of the World's' novelette style, the organisation of
headlines and other spatially associated images, such as particular
photographs on the same page, frequently produce a report, or lend
themselves to a particular reading, which detracts from the gravity
of the specific offence and thereby serves to confirm and perpetuate specific widely held cultural values concerning the general
character of rape.

In examining reports of rape we will concentrate on three
aspects of press accounts:
(a) accounts of motivation,
(b) description of characters,
(c) social control themes.

ACCOUNTS OF MOTIVATION

To a certain extent it is inevitable that press reports of rape
cases, especially when they reach court, will reflect the concerns
of the legal system and will re-present the motives for rape that
are expressed in the courtroom. In other words the court's interest in the sex-life of rape victims makes it 'legitimate' for the
press to report such details from the trial as they may consider
'newsworthy'. As the courts rarely place any restriction on
reporting this means that the press is free to print what might be
argued constitutes irrelevant and humiliating material, drawn
selectively from the information extracted from the victim by the
courts. Similarly with the question of motivation for rape, the
press often merely reproduces specific statements made in court by
legal representatives and by offenders themselves. The selected
statements reported in the press on the motivation for rape in
particular cases are problematically related to the complete court
proceedings as recorded in the court transcript. Whereas the full
transcript of a trial records the expression of dissenting points
of view, press accounts typically select particular statements that
are compatible with the specific negotiated outcome of the trial.
    Interestingly the reasons given for rape that appear in the
press are almost always taken from statements by the defending
counsel, or the judge in his summing up, or in the passing of
sentence. Less frequently 'experts' in psychology or sexual pathology are invited to pass comment but this is only in exceptional
cases, for example as in the case of the Cambridge Rapist where
Mary Whitehouse, the Chief Constable of Cambridge, the owner of a
sex-shop in Cambridge and a consultant psychiatrist were called
upon in press reports to account for the assaults. Rarely however
is the victim's or the prosecuting counsel's reasoning reported.
Consequently motivations for rape which are provided with the
specific intention of trying to achieve an acquittal for the
accused, or in an attempt to reduce his sentence, are reported in
the press as *the* motivations and therefore these statements assume
the status of legitimate and reasonable accounts of rape. Thus we
find in many newspaper accounts a version of the frustration-
aggression hypothesis in which the convicted rapist's responsibility for his behaviour is diminished either by appeal to his
'condition' as a sexually frustrated man or by reference to the
'uncontrollable' level of his sexual arousal. This kind of appeal
assumes many forms from references to the rapist's wife's pregnancy, to the period of 'enforced' sexual abstinence, to the
effect of alcohol and drugs, and to the 'problems' of adolescence.
Consider the following:
    Case 1: He drank about two gallons of beer before the attack
             outside the disco. ... The pregnancy of B's wife may
             have been 'one of the reasons for his committing the
             offence'. ('News of the World', 25 January 1976)
    Case 2: R. attacked her five days before his wife gave birth
             to their first child. ('Guardian', 25 June 1976)
    Case 3: Sex-starved window cleaner C. arrived at a young
             woman's house as she was having a bath.... C. told
             police he had not had sex for eight months. ('Sun',
             13 November 1976)

Case 4:   Two young men ... raped a 14 year old girl after
          drinking with her in a pub and a club.... It was not
          unusual for young men to take advantage of a girl or
          for young men to behave totally out of character after
          having something to drink, said the judge. ('Daily
          Mail', 19 March 1976)
Case 5:   Judge Christmas Humphreys told him ... 'Possibly at a
          difficult age (18) of your life you were overcome by
          your own sexual urges to do something you deeply regret.
          I hope this is so.' ('Daily Express', 21 June 1975)

Such newspaper reports of rape cases serve to perpetuate the
commonly held belief that rape is simply the outcome of sexual
frustration or arousal rather than an act of violence, domination
and degradation. Moreover the concentration upon specific characteristics of the individual rapist and the victim, and the unneces-
sarily detailed description of events immediately prior to, during
and after the rape, serves to create the impression that rape is
an isolated event having no structural relationship to other social
practices or phenomena, or to the unequal and exploitative character of the relationships between men and women in general.

DESCRIPTION OF CHARACTERS

The image of the rapist and the victim as re-presented in the press
varies quite considerably according to whether or not the rape
corresponds closely to the rape stereotype in terms of which the
rapist can be defined as a sexual psychopath, or whether it approx-
imates to the more complex and realistic portrayal of rape as
outlined by Amir (1971). Consider for example the press portrayal
of the 'Cambridge Rapist', convicted for assaulting eight women.
The press, almost universally, described him as an abomination, as
follows:
    'The Beast from Broadmoor gets life' ('Sun', 4 October 1975)
    'The twisted mind of hooded sex monster ... was laid bare
    yesterday' ('Daily Mirror', 4 October 1975)
    'Fantasies of the Fiend' ('Daily Express', 4 October 1975)
    'The cunning beast who terrorized a city' ('Guardian', 4
    October 1975)
Such reactions by the press are rare, however, and usually occur
only in the case of multiple rape, gang rapes, or alternatively
where the victim is either very old or very young. Such rapes as
these are more easily described in clearly defined moral terms than
those cases where the victim is 'young' and 'attractive' and the
rapist is apparently a 'normal' male. In fact even though the
majority of rapes reported in the press fit into this latter
category, the impact of mass coverage of a few notorious rapists
seems to be sufficient to sustain the general stereotype of rape.
    Where reference is made to the socio-economic class or occupa-
tion of the rapist in press reports the general impression given
is that rapists are from manual working backgrounds, the occupations referred to varying from mechanic, colliery worker, casual
labourer, to painter and to the unemployed. The majority of
rapists described in the press are white but it is significant that

where convicted rapists are black, or non-white immigrants, press
attention in the case appears to increase. It should be added
however that in the cases of R. v. Moving and R. v. Ghailam and
others, cases which provoked considerable press interest, the
controversy which followed their respective trials was in large
part a result of Judge Christmas Humphrey's and Judge Edward
Sutcliffe's remarks and sentencing policy.(8) It remains open to
speculation whether the reactions and press coverage would have
been comparable had the accused in the respective cases been
native-born whites.

Very few victims of the rapes reported in the press are non-
white. As yet it is impossible to say whether this is, or is not,
an accurate representation of the reality of rape in the UK.
Certainly, given Amir's (1971) findings in the USA that black
women are more frequently the victims of rape than white women, we
ought to be mindful of the impression created, by the absence of
reports, that black women are rarely the victims of rape attacks
or sexual assaults. We could here be within the territory of what
Brownmiller refers to as the 'male sexual fantasy', that is to say
that one of the criteria for selecting a rape case for report in
the newspaper is the 'attractiveness' of the victim. This of
course has meant, in terms of prevailing cultural values, some
combination of the following: young, tall, attractive, blonde,
brunette and white.

SOCIAL CONTROL THEMES

It has been argued that rape constitutes a form of social control
in so far as it represents a means of keeping women in 'their
place', a way of constraining their behaviour. For example
Griffin has stated that:
      The threat of rape is used to deny women employment.... The
      fear of rape keeps women off the streets at night. Keeps
      women at home. Keeps women passive and modest for fear that
      they be thought provocative. (1971, p.35)
It is not rape itself which constitutes a form of social control
but the internalisation by women, through continual socialisation,
of the possibility of rape. This implicit threat of rape is conveyed in terms of certain prescriptions which are placed upon the
behaviour of girls and women, and through the common-sense understandings which 'naturalise' gender appropriate forms of behaviour.
Both the implicit threat of rape, couched in terms of prevalent
social stereotypes, and the conventionally accepted ways to avoid
such an experience, being in some places rather than others, doing
some things but not others, adopting only specific attitudes, etc.,
are conveyed, and continually reinforced along with a whole range
of cultural values concerning female (and male) sexuality.

Newspapers constitute one source of the continual socialisation
of women, their accounts of rape serving to perpetuate and reinforce specific naturalistic assumptions and stereotypes about
women and female sexuality. The extent to which the press depicts
women as sexual objects and ignores the reality of most women's
lives, which includes economic, political and a variety of other

activities, ultimately confirms cultural values which place women
in the home, passively subordinate to men in every sphere including
sexuality. Press reports of rape, however, often serve a more
specific function than just a general reconfirmation of women's
inferior status, for in many cases there is a warning or caution
for women, such as where and when not to go for a walk, how not to
behave and what not to wear. Such warnings may be quite implicit
but none the less they serve as reminders for women of the boundaries of socially approved behaviour and sensitise them to the
possible consequences of violating social conventions.

In reports of rape in the press, as indeed in news coverage
generally, there is a serious absence of background analysis. As
a result there is a tendency for superficial details in the
sequence of events reported to become associated with the central
topic or phenomenon (e.g., drinking in a pub with a rape) and
thereby to assume the status of a causal factor. The very structure and superficiality of press accounts lend themselves to
interpretations or readings of the behaviour which may have given
rise to an opportunity for rape as actually precipitating the
assault. In other words the selective reporting of the facts in a
particular rape case, concerning for example the scene of the
assault, the circumstances leading the participants into the
specific location, as well as the behaviour directly preceding the
rape, produces a text which by connotation conveys a sense of the
causal character of merely associated factors. A necessary aspect
of such texts is their reliance upon specific dimensions of conventional understandings of rape (where, when and how women get
raped) for these provide the structure through which the 'story' is
told.

In so far as a press report of rape never seeks to explain or
address the existence of the general phenomenon of rape but merely
selectively focuses on a specific instance, the account which is
produced is structured in terms of the surface details of the
specific case concerned. As a result the underlying structuring of
social and sexual relations, which both produce the possibility of
rape and make specific social locations and circumstances likely
venues for rape, remain undisclosed in press accounts. Thereby the
conventional wisdoms concerning rape are upheld, namely that women
who get raped are in some sense responsible for their own fate,
could in fact have avoided their suffering by not putting themselves
at risk by entering the specific social space or territory within
which the rape occurred. Consider the following examples from
press reports:

Case 1:   Raped hiker imprudent (headline)
          [A court] suspended two of the four years' imprisonment
          imposed on a motorist convicted of raping a girl hitch-
          hiker because his responsibility was 'diminished' by
          the fact that the girl had, in effect, solicited him by
          getting into his car. ('Guardian', 15 April 1976)

Case 2:   The woman aged 28 accepted a lift from them after a
          dance....
               The alleged offences took place after she was driven
          to R's house. ('Sun', 15 January 1976)

Case 3:   Two brothers who made a 'callous and brutal' sexual
          attack on two girl students ... admitted picking up
          [the] girls hitch-hiking outside Warwick University.
          ('Guardian', 30 September 1976)

Case 4:   (Defending counsel) said: 'This girl was unwise to let
          him into the house wearing only a dressing gown.'
          ('Sun', 13 November 1976)

Case 5:   Two young men ... raped a 14-year-old girl after
          drinking with her in a pub and a club. ('Daily Mail',
          19 March 1976)

In this way press reports may be regarded as implicitly cautioning
women as to where they go, what they wear and how they behave.

The cumulative effect of press reports of rape is to remind
women of their vulnerability, to create an atmosphere of fear and
to suggest, as a solution, that women should withdraw to the
traditional shelter of the domestic sphere and the protection of
their men. For example, in the words of one Chief Inspector of
Police, 'I don't wish to appear alarmist, but women and girls who
are forced to walk alone should take a route where there are
plenty of people about, even if it means going out of their way'
('Star' (Sheffield), 26 June 1976). In other words women are to
limit their freedom in order to avoid rape. The irony of this kind
of advice and the related representation of rape in the media is
that they are based on a false premise. Namely that rape is an
isolated, socially unstructured phenomenon which affects specific
categories of women in special social circumstances. The reality
is significantly different, however, for rape may take place within
the domestic sphere, among family and friends, as much as amongst
strangers. Hence rape becomes a form of social control in a dual
sense, first, inasmuch as it is a form of physical coercion and
violence, and second, in so far as the fear or threat of rape, as
communicated by the media, in literature, on film and in the press,
serves to socialise women into tacitly constraining and limiting
their own forms of behaviour and social activity.

NOTES

1 Joan Little killed a prison guard in Beaufort county jail (USA)
   as he was trying to rape her, while Inez Garcia shot one of
   two men who raped her 17 minutes *after* she had been raped.
   Both cases raised the vital issue of whether a woman has the
   right to defend herself from a sexual assault.

2 The case involving Judge Christmas Humphreys was R. v. Moving
   (June 1975). In this case the young man who pleaded guilty to
   raping two women at knifepoint was sentenced to six months'
   jail on each charge, suspended for two years. In R. v. Ghailam
   and Others, five Moroccan youths, aged thirteen to eighteen
   years, were convicted of repeatedly raping a girl of twenty.
   Judge Edward Sutcliffe sentenced two of them to Borstal, one to
   a detention centre for six months, one was put into the care of
   the Local Authority and the fifth was remanded for sentence and
   ultimately given a three-year prison sentence. Both of these
   cases aroused public concern because of the leniency of the
   sentences imposed on the rapists.

3   Cf. the case of J.C., who had been jailed for two years for
    raping the wife of a friend and who was then freed on appeal by
    Lord Justice Lawton because it was held that his original con-
    viction had been on the grounds that his belief that the woman
    consented was *unreasonable*. ('The Times', 24 May 1975).
4   This publication includes special chapters for women on how to
    avoid attack within the home and in public.
5   The so-called Cambridge Rapist assaulted eight women in
    Cambridge over a period of eight months between October 1974
    and June 1975. He was a total stranger to his victims whom he
    treated with considerable violence and brutality and in none of
    his attacks was there (nor could there be) any suggestion that
    the victim was 'responsible' for being raped.
6   For example in a case reported in the 'News of the World', 31
    October 1971, the accused, although found guilty, was to a
    certain extent exonerated because the trial judge held that he
    had been provoked by the blonde victim.
7   In particular her reference to the rape scenes in 'Town Without
    Pity' and 'Last Summer'.
8   See note 2.

8 Studying rape
Integrating research and social change

Julia R. Schwendinger and Herman Schwendinger

The summer of 1971 was rapidly approaching and the incidence of
rape was already on the rise in the city of Berkeley. Activities
were beginning to change, but Berkeley at that time still remained
a focal point, training ground, and inspiration for white, radical
student movements in other cities. The colourful political
behaviour of its students and street people was a source of
frequent national news reportage. Its Free Speech Movement and
People's Park struggles against the university, which was a symbol
of thought-control and corporate landlordship; and its anti-war
activities, which were highlighted by marches, strikes, rock-
throwing, bombing and burning attempts, and which were aimed
against national policies, university property, local businessmen
and police tactics, served as a magnet for apolitical as well as
radical youth with many reasons for 'digging' the Berkeley scene.

The year 1970 in Berkeley had marked a high point of 110
officially reported rapes and a steadily rising trend of rape
rates. Arrest rates, on the other hand, showed a much slower
increase. A category of women believed to be particularly vulnerable, the summer transients and visitors to exciting Berkeley, was
already arriving. Young women and men from all over the country
were filling the sidewalks of Telegraph Avenue which had become a
young people's meeting place, and flooding into the Free Clinic, as
a place where free medical and emotional attention could be sought
and found. Some became members of the Women's Health Collective
where a woman could participate in an effective paramedical helping
role. The problems of rape victims repeatedly came to their
attention.

Those who first helped organise the rape crisis work included
two women with families, who represented a relatively traditional
lifestyle. However, the younger women who were interested in
Health Collective and anti-rape activities had migrated during the
late 1960s from colleges and homes in cities all over the country.
In spite of their dress, which was characterised by 'farmer johns',
blue jeans with patches, second-hand store vintage 'funky' blouses;
and in spite of their hair being 'natural', that is, not 'set', and
sometimes uncombed, their backgrounds were solidly middle-class and
professional.

The class background and attraction of the group were clear in many of its characteristics, but the conscious motive of many of the members was to make a break with middle-class relationships and to live like the working class, or at least according to their perceptions of the working class. An effort was made to relate to working-class and third-world women. For some there were also the vicissitudes of living on welfare. And with this objectively declassed status, there came the personal exposure to victimisation which always characterises the lives of poor women.

To meet the needs of young women who were part of this wave of travellers, women from the Health Collective and members of the Medical Committee for Human Rights spoke in the Community Theatre at a Berkeley City Council meeting where community health proposals were being heard. In statements marked by eloquence and poignancy, a demand was raised for a woman's health centre, part of which was to be a twenty-four-hour rape crisis centre. The enormous and friendly community audience (the City of Berkeley was experiencing a unique stage of community involvement) that had gathered in town-hall fashion was told how the victim was treated at the local Hospital, where she was taken following her report that a rape had taken place. Then we were given a sense of what Berkeley police attitudes were like:

'Berkeley police regard rape as the woman's fault. [They claim that] you were hitch-hiking and you left your door unlocked ... you were waiting for a bus late at night.... [thus] confirming the false consciousness that women are inferior. The victim is turned into a criminal and very little is done to catch the rapist....'

After describing the police attitudes towards victims, the speakers voiced a set of demands. The philosophy behind their statements emphasised the need for alternative services.

'The women of Berkeley will not stand for this situation any longer, we demand that the City Council pass the proposal for a women's health center where a woman can get supportive medical and psychological care. Such a center would also train women in self-defense and keep a central file on all rapists' descriptions, car makes, and methods of attack. This information would then be circulated in the community and hopefully Berkeley will become a place which all rapists will become wary of because of our community action.'

From the audience there were shouts of 'Right on!'

The Berkeley City Council never approved funds for a rape crisis centre, but the group that was to become Bay Area Women Against Rape (BAWAR) essentially emerged a few months after this meeting. Also, beginning with our attendance at this meeting, the initial stage of the field research discussed in this paper was 'officially' under way. It had previously been decided that research, whose goal was generating knowledge about the crime, and also knowledge about the official treatment of the victim, would be an important contribution to the struggle against rape. However, our purpose was not to generate technical information for its own sake about incidence, arrest and imprisonment rates. Although the latter has been an important aim among professionals in our field, the former aim - making a contribution to the struggle of women against rape -

had not, to our knowledge, as yet been achieved by other criminologists.

With regard to the subject area of rape, in 1970 the university of California's Berkeley library had been scoured for material. There was virtually no information published. What there was lay concealed in professional literature: law journal articles, psychoanalytic analyses, social control writings about offenders and victimology writings where the emphasis was on blaming the victim. There was very little of theoretical worth and nothing on the methodology of rape research.

In studies of the criminal justice system, rape was either ignored altogether or dealt with summarily. One otherwise extremely perceptive researcher, William Westley (1971), interviewed police and, oblivious to their discriminatory sexist practices, uncritically accepted their myths about the numerous false claims and the notions that rape victims have ulterior motives. He stated that:

> [Police] have to be very careful since many complaints are made to police as camouflage for other actions or needs. Thus, the young girl or woman who wants some publicity may claim to have been raped. A mother who is angry at one of her daughter's boyfriends may claim that he has attacked her girl. A woman anxious to hurt some man may claim that he raped her. (Westley, 1971, p.62)

This writer admitted that the police 'know that they have no evidence' in sex cases; yet he ignored the implications of this admission. If the police do not, then the author himself could not have the data to warrant his generalisation. In our opinion, he was insufficiently critical in accepting the police officer's assumptions about the veracity of rape victims.

Since 1971, because of the influence of feminist movements and feminist writings, researchers on the victim of rape and the criminal justice system have attempted to break out of the traditional conservative mould. But traditions can be maintained by women as well as men. Two women researchers (Burgess and Holstrom, 1974) in 1972 offered a crisis intervention service to Boston City Hospital, if the hospital would phone them each time a rape victim was admitted. Their study was based on these cases. As a manual for 'crisis workers' their book on the rape victim is fine but since the authors were not in an independent advocacy relation to the institution, their research became highly accommodative. Aside from a few suggestions (e.g., the hospital should give free examinations), the hospital as well as the police were given a clean bill of health. They published no sharp criticisms of the treatment variations that are mediated, almost everywhere in America, by the sex, race and class of the patients. With a total lack of any political perspective, criticism of the police was replaced by apology. 'Police', they stated, 'are on the side of the victim more than any other professional group. They are the one solid group of professionals who see case after case and see what happens to victims...' (Burgess and Holstrom, 1974, p.78). Undoubtedly there are some supportive police officers but police injustice and corruption are well known in sexual as well as fiscal matters.

THE RESEARCH

This accommodative stance may be more successfully avoided in
advocacy research, when institutional functions are evaluated
directly in relation to the needs of people requesting service.
The needs of a bureaucracy itself are given less priority. As a
result, a more comprehensive evaluation of the functions of institutions is made possible. This evaluation usually encourages
researchers to question the forces that determine basic institutional operations.

   Whether these forces are adequately understood, however,
depends upon the choice of social theory and political standpoint.
A methodology alone does not ensure that the researcher will ask
the right questions or arrive at an analysis that is critical of
basic causal social relations. Researchers with a deep commitment
to the status quo would not perform advocacy research, but if they
did, their establishment connections, theoretical as well as
professional, would prevent their 'biting the hand that feeds them'.
In our case, Marxian theories, which analyse institutions within
the framework of our political economy as a whole, provided us with
important insights into rape and the treatment of the victim of
rape. The Marxian concept of praxis has also been helpful,
because it encourages researchers to become actively involved in
changing human institutions as well as studying them critically.

   Furthermore, active participation in a movement to change the
institutions that treat rape victims was maintained simultaneously
with our efforts to understand the research problem at hand.
During the fall of 1971 in the first phase of the field research,
for example, we used traditional questionnaire methods to obtain
information about the treatment of rape victims. Several hundred
questionnaires were distributed to large lecture classes at a
university. The distribution was preceded by a talk on rape and
by an announcement that an anti-rape group for women was in the
process of formation. (Many members of the early, working nucleus
of the group were recruited from among the women who responded to
these lectures.) Since, presumably, most of the women who received
the questionnaires had not been raped, a large return was not
expected. But thirty-four rape victims did respond to the
questions, which covered such diverse areas as socio-economic
status of the victim's family, conditions under which the rape took
place, victim's relationship to the offender, approximation of the
offender's occupation or socio-economic status, type and amount of
force used, type and amount of resistance the victim employed,
whether the rape was reported to the police, whether the victim
sought medical or psychological treatment, the victim's experiences
with police, doctors, DAs, defense attorneys, and judges, and the
emotional after-effects. Finally, the questionnaires asked whether
the women would consent to an interview.

   The next source of information was the personal interview.
Twenty-seven taped in-depth interviews which lasted on the average
of ninety minutes each were gathered. Some interviews were
obtained from questionnaire responses; most others were referred.
For example, a victim who responded favourably to an interview
would refer us to other women who had been raped.

The forty hours of taped material sensitised us to the feelings
and characteristics of the women. Some of the victims regarded the
interview as an opportunity to do something which might be helpful
in dealing with the rape problem; some experienced a feeling of
purging themselves from a previously undisclosed yet still nagging
problem. Another special set of interviews, recorded and
excerpted onto a tape for public education, with the help of other
members of the anti-rape group, provided additional insights.

The methods of an ethnographer as well as those of the activist-
observer in a woman's anti-rape group, contributed immeasurably to
our understanding of the nature of the problems. Julia's participation in the group as a founding member and, for three years, as a
victim's advocate (1) served as an important source of sensitising
information. Over the period of time that Julia served as a
victim's advocate, the group responded to the reports and requests
of several hundred women who had been molested - either subjected
to rape or to attempted rape. Many of these cases were discussed
in the group for the purpose of sharing information, and for
advising and supporting the individual woman whose turn it was to
respond to the call for help by the victim. The extensive variation in both types of cases and conditions under which rape occurs,
and in the multitude of problems faced by the victims, was dramatically demonstrated in this process.

When the research began, formal and informal discussions with
police officers evidenced stereotypic notions about rape victims
as well as 'public relations' statements about police-victim
contracts, which contrasted strongly with the victims' reports we
had been hearing. In addition, as a member of an activist group,
Julia was able to participate directly in several meetings with
upper echelon police. At that time the police tried to rationalise
specific mistreatment of victims by placing blame on an individual
officer and not on departmental policy. In a self-serving fashion,
they made clear that the group members, as lay people, could not
be expected to understand professionals' problems. Had there been
no opportunities to compare police interview responses with the
realities of criminal justice operations, obtained from ongoing
practical efforts to change the system, it would have been impossible to distinguish very precisely between a 'public relations
response' from police officers and an accurate account of department operations. Also, without this type of comparison it would
have been impossible to spot the causal relationships which lie
beyond the awareness of the institutional authorities. Thus,
regarding the understanding of the criminal justice system, direct
practice in a woman's advocacy group proved *most* valuable.

Rape victims requesting aid clarified their treatment by the
criminal justice system. The weight of their statements and
complaints indicated that the victims' treatment was not, as
claimed by police at a meeting, the fault of one or two scapegoat
policemen. In fact we came to understand, from victims' statements, the way women were being treated by police better than the
head of a department or a police chief could estimate by simply
perusing the reports written by individual officers who were
unconscious of their own biases.

Another aspect of the anti-rape group's practice which provided

information involved monitoring trials, discussing and criticising
them with the victims and the DAs. No amount of interviewing
lawyers or judges would have demonstrated the dynamics effecting
the sexist treatment accorded victims in court. Trips made by
members to Sacramento, where new rape legislation was under consideration, revealed sexism among law-makers and their over-concern
about such infrequent cases as a prostitute's reporting rape after
a customer refuses to pay. Legislators' ignorance of the way
victims are treated and of the way women respond emotionally to
being raped, and their ignorance of the sexism built into well-
established law, was demonstrated at these open hearings. Subsequent experiences while working with the victims' problems
indicated sexist treatment emanating from hospital policy and
medical personnel.

The response of hospital medical administrators and doctors was
hostile. The attitude of these medical personnel was that the
group's representatives were lay people and should mind their own
business. The medical personnel were very status and money oriented. To them, the group members were mere community women; and
because of medical training, the doctor's behaviour was not to be
questioned. The social distance between the group members and the
hospital personnel was so great, that they did not even bother
with public relations statements. Bad treatment was simply a
mistaken judgment by an individual doctor. It was their contention
that the policies of the hospital were to treat women and rape
victims just like anyone else. If this was true then everybody was
being mistreated by hospital personnel. On the other hand, women
of varying types received differential treatment from the police:
some women, who were raped by strangers, often found the police
were not as bad as they had expected. However, the women who went
to the hospital almost *invariably* complained about callous treatment.

To defend the women who received treatment at the hospital, the
group directly engaged in a struggle with the hospital authorities
to change emergency room procedures. Simultaneously, it particip-
ated in a coalition with other community health groups to prevent
the hospital from being granted a million and a half dollars from
a federal agency for a community mental health programme. The
grant was blocked and the hospital authorities began to re-evaluate
their institution's relationship to the community. In addition,
another outcome of the struggle was that the director of medical
services in the emergency room was replaced by a more sympathetic
person who instituted the new procedures.

The practices of defending women in such institutional settings
as police headquarters, the courts, the hospitals and the legislature, provided further correct information about the forces that
determined institutional operations. It encouraged the development
of a more accurate perspective than would have been acquired had
we simply used typical social science theories and methods. It is
our opinion that 'activist-observation', conducted while participating in a women's advocacy group, for example, represents a
superior technique for understanding our social institutions. It
is possible only through struggle to understand the parameters of
the criminal justice system. The struggle to change these social
institutions generates circumstances that make it possible for

committed observers to gain profound insights into the workings of
the system.

Participation in a woman's advocacy group therefore affected the
course of the research. Various goals developed in the course of
the work. In the early part of the research, discovering the variations in the treatment of rape victims by such institutions as the
police, the hospitals and the courts became a chief focus of
investigation. A second goal was disseminating the information to
victims, other women and the general public. Finally, a third
goal involved developing an ongoing victim advocacy programme with
other women. The main purpose of this activity was to minimise the
negative effects on the victim, to monitor and change the practices
of the institution, and to develop strategies for prevention, at
the least cost to already oppressed people. Because of the participation in developing the goals of the programme, the programme's
goals and our goals came to overlap. As a result of this identity
of interests, the usual bourgeois differentiation between theory
and practice, which is signified by such terms as 'pure theory' and
'applied theory', disappeared.

SOCIAL CHANGE

In this process, far more was accomplished than merely uncovering
information about sexism in the medical and criminal justice
systems; the methodology, after all, requires activism as well as
observation. A number of reforms were wrought in the treatment of
the victim. More humane treatment including gentle examinations,
privacy, showers and information about possible effects of the
assault, are now offered by some hospitals. There are police
departments where officers are especially trained for relating
sympathetically and effectively to rape victims. Various items
of legislation and legal precedents, eliminating the mandatory
cautionary note and reducing the number of situations in which the
victim's sex-life can be exposed in open court, have become established. Despite these improvements, however, much more fundamental
changes must be made. Our practice revealed the magnitude of the
problems of such victims in relation to society as a whole.

Rape is one of the most significant forms of victimising women
in our society, but it is not represented by socially isolated
acts. Because the sexist, racist and class-linked modes of oppression that lead men to this act actually permeate all parts of
society, rape and the fear of rape are related to myriad everyday
interactions between men and women. To understand these modes, it
is necessary to deal with the material causes of sexist doctrines,
and the effects of these doctrines on the victim, the rapist, and
the personnel in the medical and criminal justice systems. It is
also necessary to recognise that male chauvinism is often conjoined
with other chauvinistic practices that maintain manifold forms of
social inequality.

Sexist doctrines, which are combined with chauvinistic ideolog-
ies, and an exploitative class-divided society (which is determined
by the capitalist mode of production) are key elements in the
causes of rape and the treatment of rape victims today. Historical

features of sexism and its pervasiveness operate through myth,
religion and women's roles in production and reproduction. The
structurally determined role of women in the family and the
economy are contributory factors to the development and the maintenance of sexism among rapists, doctors and professionals who
function in the courts.

The recipients of sexist treatment are not equally distributed.
Today, women who conform to a stereotyped image of the middle-class
or upper-class 'good woman' type are usually well-treated by
police. They also represent a smaller number of the official rape
population. Other women who do not conform - who are poor, third
world, lesbians, hippies or prostitutes - are generally derogated
and considered non-rapable. Yet they comprise the majority of the
official rapes even though their numerical strength is reduced by
police and prosecutorial discretion and by defence 'sexual smear'
tactics.

Another significant population of rape victims emerges during
imperialist wars and under fascism. Recent examples include rape
as an instrument of torture in Chile and in the Vietnamese War,
and rape as a means for terrorising and subduing a rebellious
population in the Pakistani-Bangladesh War. In addition to the
structural determinants of rape within our own country, the instit-
utionalisation of rape elsewhere by military and political authorities signifies the futility of meliorative strategies alone, for
the elimination of this crime. The treatment of rape victims can
be affected by women's advocacy groups. But rape itself can only
be eliminated when deterrence measures are conjoined with a
socialist strategy for social change.

NOTES

1 The term 'victim's advocate' refers to a community woman,
   trained by a 'woman against rape group' in various medical,
   legal and emotional aspects of rape. The advocates are available to a rape victim to offer information and support in
   meeting any needs she may have as an outcome of rape or attempted
   rape. An advocate will accompany the victim to the police
   station, hospital and courts, if the victim so desires. The
   advocate is usually contacted initially by a phone call from a
   rape victim (occasionally a surrogate called). The victim or
   her surrogate describes the situation and asks for some form of
   assistance - usually a supportive listener, legal advice,
   whether or not to report to the police. The advocate makes
   suggestions and offers to go to the police or hospital with the
   victim who has chosen to file a police report. In cases where
   the victim complains about her treatment by the police or hospital, several members of the group see the supervisory personnel to register this complaint. On many occasions, the complaints involve sexist treatment, for instance, being prejudged
   as a 'loose woman'.

Bibliography

ACTON, W. (1857), 'The Function and Disorders of the Reproductive Organs', London, John Churchill.

ACTON, W. (1870), 'Prostitution', 2nd edn, reprinted and abridged, London, MacGibbon & Kee, 1968.

ADAMS, C. and LAURIKIETIS, R. (1976), 'The Gender Trap; Book Three Messages and Images', London, Virago.

ADLER, F. (1975), 'Sisters in Crime: The Rise of the New Female Criminal', New York, McGraw-Hill.

ADVISORY GROUP ON THE LAW OF RAPE (1975), 'Report of the Advisory Group on the Law of Rape', London, HMSO.

ALDRIDGE-MORRIS, R. (1969), An Analysis of the Personality Structure of Approved School Girls, 'Approved School Gazette', no.63, April, pp.18-25.

ALTHUSSER, L. (1971), 'Lenin and Philosophy and Other Essays', London, New Left Books.

AMIR, M. (1967), Victim Precipitated Forcible Rape, 'Journal of Criminal Law, Criminology and Police Science', vol.58, no.4.

AMIR, M. (1971), 'Patterns in Forcible Rape', University of Chicago Press.

ANDERSON, E.A. (1976), The 'Chivalrous' Treatment of the Female Offender in the Arms of the Criminal Justice System: A Review of the Literature, 'Social Problems', vol.23, no.3.

AUBERT, V. (ed.) (1972), 'Sociology of Law', Harmondsworth, Penguin.

BECKER, H. et al. (1961), 'Boys in White: Student Culture in Medical School', University of Chicago Press.

BENGTSSON, M. (1969), The Political Economy of Women's Liberation, 'Monthly Review', September.

BEWLEY, B.R., and BEWLEY, T.H. (1975), Hospital Doctor's Career Structure and Misuse of Medical Womanpower, 'The Lancet', 9 August.

BIRT, J. and JAY, P. (1975), Television Journalism: the Child of an Unhappy Marriage between Newspapers and Film, 'The Times', 30 September.

BLOS, P. (1957), Preoedipal Factors in the Etiology of Female Delinquency, 'Psychoanalytic Study of the Child', vol.12, pp.229-49.

BRECHER, R. and BRECHER, E. (1966), 'An Analysis of Human Sexual Response', New York, Signet Books.

BROWNMILLER, S. (1975), 'Against Our Will: Men, Women and Rape', London, Secker & Warburg.
BURGESS, Ann Wolbert and HOLMSTROM, Lynda Lytle (1974), 'Rape: Victims of Crises', Maryland, Robert J. Brady.
CHESLER, P. (1972), 'Women and Madness', New York, Doubleday.
CHESNEY-LIND, M. (1973), Judicial Enforcement of the Female Sex Role: The Family Court and the Female Delinquent, 'Issues in Criminology', vol.8, no.2.
CHRISTIE, N. (1975), 'Hvor teet et samfunn?' ('A Closely Knit Society?'), Copenhagen/Oslo, Chr. Ejlers/Universitetsforlaget.
CHRISTIE, V. (1976), Den tredobbelt kontrollerede (The Triple Controlled), 'Kriminalpolitik', 2 and 3, Copenhagen.
CICOUREL, A. (1968), 'Social Organization of Juvenile Justice', New York, Wiley.
CLOWARD, R.A. and OHLIN, L.E. (1961), 'Delinquency and Opportunity', London, Routledge & Kegan Paul.
COMFORT, A. (1967), 'The Anxiety Makers', London, Nelson.
CONNELL, N. and WILSON, C. (eds) (1974), 'Rape: The First Source-book for Women', New York, Plume Books.
COOTE, A. and GILL, T. (1974), 'Women's Rights: A Practical Guide', Harmondsworth, Penguin.
COOTE, A. and GILL, T. (1975), 'The Rape Controversy', London, NCCL.
COUSSINS, J. (1976), 'The Equality Report', London, NCCL.
COWIE, J., COWIE, V. and SLATER, E. (1968), 'Delinquency in Girls', London, Heinemann.
CRIME PREVENTION DEPARTMENT (1976), 'Violent Crime and You', Avon and Somerset Constabulary.
DAHL, T. Stang et al. (1975), 'Juss og Juks: En arbeidsbok i likestilling' ('Law and Trickery, A Manual in Equality'), Oslo, Pax.
DAHL, T. Stang (1976), Ekteskapet, den moderne husmannskontrakten, (Marriage, the Modern Contract of Feudal Legacy), 'Kvinnekunnskap' ('Women's Knowledge'), (eds) T. Støren and T.S. Wetlesen, Oslo, Gyldendal.
DAHL, T. Stang (1977), 'Barnevern og samfunnsvern', ('Child Welfare and Social Defence'), Oslo, Pax.
DALLA COSTA, M. and JAMES, S. (1973), 'The Power of Women and the Subversion of the Community', Bristol, Falling Wall Press.
DAVIES, J. and GOODMAN, N. (1972), 'Girl Offenders Aged 17-20 Years', Home Office Research Unit Report, London, HMSO.
DAVIS, K. (1937), The Sociology of Prostitution, 'American Sociological Review', vol.2, pp.744-55.
DEACON, A. and HILL, M. (1972), 'The Problem of Surplus Women in the Nineteenth Century: Secular and Religious Alternative', in A Sociological Yearbook of Religion in Britain, vol.5, London, Student Christian Movement Press.
de BEAUVOIR, S. (1972), 'The Second Sex', Harmondsworth, Penguin.
DINITZ, S., RECKLESS, W., SCARPITTI, F. and MURRAY, E. (1960), The Good Boy in a High Delinquent Area, 'American Sociological Review', vol.25.
DOWNES, D.H. (1966), 'The Delinquent Solution', London, Routledge & Kegan Paul.
DUREA, M.A. and ASSUM, A. (1948), Reliability of Personality Traits Differentiating Delinquent and Non-Delinquent Girls, 'Journal of Genetic Psychology', vol.72, p.307-11.

EDMOND, W. and FLEMING, S. (eds) (1975), 'All Work and No Pay:
Women, Housework and the Wages Due', Bristol, Falling Wall Press
and Power of Women Collective.
EHRENREICH, B. and ENGLISH, D. (1974), 'Witches, Midwives and
Nurses: A History of Women Healers', London, Compendium.
ELLIS, H. (1936), 'Studies in the Psychology of Sex', vol.IV,
ch.vii, Prostitution, New York, Random House.
ENSTAD, K. et al. (1974), Kvinner og kriminalstatistikh (Women and
Criminal Statistics), unpublished paper, Institute of Criminology
and Criminal Law, University of Oslo.
ERIKSSON, L.D. (1976), Kritisk rettsteori som ideologikritikk
(Critical Legal Theory as Ideological Criticism), in Brathom and
Sundby (eds), 'Kritisk Juss' ('Critical Law'), Oslo, Pax.
EQUALITY WORKING PARTY OF THE NATIONAL UNION OF JOURNALISTS (1975),
'Images of Women', London, NUJ.
FARROW, L. (1974), The Independent Woman and the Cinema of Rape, in
N. Connell and C. Wilson (eds.), 'Rape: The First Sourcebook for
Women', New York, Plume Books.
FINSTAD, L. (1975), Kjønnet avgjordge - kvinnene fikk sparken, (The
Sex Decided - the Women were Fired), unpublished paper, Institute
of Ethnography, University of Oslo.
FISHER, S. (1973), 'Understanding the Female Orgasm', Harmondsworth,
Penguin.
FLYVEL, T.R. (1963), 'The Insecure Offender', London, Chatto &
Windus.
FORD, C.S. and BEACH, F.A. (1951), 'Patterns of Sexual Behaviour',
New York, Harper.
FREIDAN, B. (1972), 'The Feminine Mystique', Harmondsworth, Penguin.
FREUD, S. (1905), Three Essays on the Theory of Sexuality, in 'The
Standard Edition of the Complete Psychological Works of Sigmund
Freud', vol.7, London, Hogarth Press.
FREUD, S. (1973), 'Introductory Lectures on Psychoanalysis',
Harmondsworth, Penguin.
GAGNON, J.H. and SIMON, W. (1974), 'Sexual Conduct: The Social
Sources of Human Sexuality', London, Hutchinson.
GALBRAITH, J.K. (1973), The Economics of the American Housewife,
'Atlantic Monthly', vol.232, no.2, pp.78-83.
GALLIHER, J.F. (1973), The Influence of Funding Agencies on
Juvenile Delinquency Research, 'Social Problems', vol.21.
GARDINER, J. (1975), Women's Domestic Labour, 'New Left Review', 89.
GARDINER, J. (1976), Political Economy of domestic labour in
Capitalist Society, in D. Leonard Barker and S. Allen (eds),
'Dependence and Exploitation in Work and Marriage', London, Longman.
GILLEY, J. (1974), How to Help the Raped, 'New Society', vol.28,
no.612.
GLEN, J. and KAPLAN, E.H. (1968), Types of Orgasm in Women: A
Critical Review and Redefinition, 'Journal of the American Psycho-
analytical Association', vol.16, no.3.
GOFFMAN, E. (1961), 'Asylums', New York, Doubleday.
GOLD, M. (1970), 'Delinquent Behaviour in an American City',
Belmont, Brook.
GORER, G. (1973), 'Sex and Marriage in Britain', London, Panther.
GOSLIN, D.A. (1969), 'Handbook of Socialization Theory and Research',
Chicago, Rand MacNally.

GRAHAM, H. (1976a), Images of Pregnancy in Ante-Natal Literature, unpublished paper presented at the British Sociological Association Annual Conference, April.
GRAHAM, H. (1976b), Women's Attitudes to Conception and Pregnancy, unpublished paper presented at the Eugenics Society Symposium on Equalities and Inequalities in Family Life, September.
GRATUS, J. (1975), Rape: Do You Ask For It?, 'Over 21', August, p.72.
GREENWOOD, V. and YOUNG, J. (1976), 'Abortion in Demand', London, Pluto.
GRIFFIN, S. (1971), Rape: the All-American Crime, 'Ramparts', September.
HASTINGS, D.W. (1966), Can Specific Training Procedures Overcome Sexual Inadequacy?, in R. Brecher and E. Brecher (eds), 'An Analysis of Human Sexual Response', New York, Signet Books.
HEIDENSOHN, F. (1968), The Deviance of Women: a Critique and an Enquiry, 'British Journal of Sociology', vol.19, no.2.
HENRIQUES, F. (1968), 'Prostitution and Society: Modern Sexuality', London, MacGibbon & Kee.
HERSCHBERGER, R. (1970), 'Adam's Rib', New York, Harper & Row.
HOFFMAN-BUSTAMANTE, D. (1973), The Nature of Female Criminality, 'Issues in Criminology', vol.8, no.2.
HØJER, R. (1974), 'Ekteskap og Forsørgelse', ('Marriage and Support'), The Commission on Equal Rights, Oslo.
IL COLLETTIVO INTERNAZIONALE FEMMINISTA (1975), 'Le operaie della casa, salario al lavoro domestico: strategia internazionale femminista' ('The Houseworkers, Pay for Housework: International Feminist Strategy'), Venice/Padua, Marsilio Editori.
JONES, E. (1923), 'Papers on Psychoanalysis', 3rd edn, London, Ballière.
KEMP, M. et al. (1975), 'Battered Women and the Law', London, Inter-Action Advisory Service Handbook 3.
KINSEY, A.C., POMEROY, W.B. and MARTIN, C.E. (1948), 'Sexual Behaviour in the Human Male', London, W.B. Saunders.
KINSEY, A.C., POMEROY, W.B., MARTIN, C.E. and GEBHARD, P.H. (1953), 'Sexual Behaviour in the Human Female', London, W.B. Saunders.
KLASS, A. (1975), 'There's Gold in them thar Pills', Harmondsworth, Penguin.
KLEIN, D. (1973), The Etiology of Female Crime: a Review of the Literature, 'Issues in Criminology', vol.8, no.2.
KLEIN, D. and KRESS, J. (1976), Any Woman's Blues: A Critical Overview of Women, Crime, and the Criminal Justics System, 'Crime and Social Justice', vol.5.
KLEIN, V. (1946), 'The Feminine Character', London, Routledge & Kegan Paul.
KONOPKA, G. (1966), 'The Adolescent Girl in Conflict', New Jersey, Prentice Hall.
LAING, R.D. (1965), 'The Divided Self', Harmondsworth, Penguin.
LAKOFF, R. (1975), 'Language and Woman's Place', New York, Harper & Row.
LAND, H. (1976), Women: Supporters or Supported? in D. Leonard Barker and S. Allen (eds), 'Sexual Divisions and Society: Process and Change', London, Tavistock.

LIND, B. Bergerson (1969), Skadede ofre for vold i Oslo (Victims of Violence in Oslo), 'Nordisk Tidsskrift for Kriminalvidenskab', ('Scandinavian Review of Penal Society'), pp.207-22.

LOMBROSO, C. and FERRERO, W. (1895), 'The Female Offender', London, Fisher Unwin.

LYKKJEN, A.M. (1976), 'Voldtekt og Kvinneundertrykking', ('Rape and Oppression'), Oslo, Pax.

MACCOBY, E. (ed.) (1966), 'The Development of Sex Differences', Stanford University Press.

MACDONALD, R.H. (1967), The Frightful Consequences of Onanism, 'Journal of the History of Ideas', vol.28, pp.423-31.

MACINTYRE, S. (1976), Who Wants Babies? The Social Construction of 'Instincts', in D. Leonard Barker and S. Allen (eds), 'Sexual Divisions and Society: Process and Change', London, Tavistock.

MCROBBIE, A. and GARBER, J. (1975), Girls and Subcultures: An Exploration, in 'Resistance Through Rituals, Cultural Studies vol. 7/8', Centre for Contemporary Cultural Studies, Birmingham University.

MARCUS, S. (1966), 'The Other Victorians: A Study of Sexuality and Pornography in Mid-Nineteenth-Century England', London, Weidenfeld & Nicolson.

MASTERS, W.H. and JOHNSON, V.E. (1966), 'Human Sexual Response', Boston, Little, Brown.

MATZA, D. (1969), 'Becoming Deviant', New Jersey, Prentice Hall.

MEAD, M. (1935), 'Sex and Temperament in Three Primitive Societies', New York, William Morrow.

MILLMAN, M. (1975), She Did it All for Love: A Feminist View of the Sociology of Deviance, in M. Millman and R. Kanter (eds), 'Another Voice', New York, Anchor Books.

MILLS, C. Wright (1959), 'The Sociological Imagination', Oxford University Press.

MITCHELL, J. (1974), 'Psychoanalysis and Feminism', London, Allen Lane.

MORGAN, D. (1975), 'Social Theory and the Family', London, Routledge & Kegan Paul.

MORRIS, R. (1964), Female Delinquency and Relational Problems, 'Social Forces', vol.43, no.1.

MUNGHAM, G. (1976), Youth in Pursuit of Itself in G. Mungham and G. Pearson (eds), 'Working Class Youth Culture', London, Routledge & Kegan Paul.

NYE, F. (1959), 'Family Relationship and Delinquent Behaviour', New York, Wiley.

OAKLEY, A. (1972), 'Sex, Gender and Society', London, Temple Smith.

OAKLEY, A. (1976), Wisewoman and Medicine Man: Changes in the Management of Childbirth, in J. Mitchell and A. Oakley (eds), 'The Rights and Wrongs of Women', Harmondsworth, Penguin.

PARKES, B. Raynier (1865), 'Essays on Women's Work', London, Alexander Strachen.

PIZZEY, E. (1974), 'Scream Quietly or the Neighbours Will Hear', Harmondsworth, Penguin.

POLLAK, O. (1961), 'The Criminality of Women', New York, A.S. Barnes.

QUICK, P. (1972), Women's Work, 'The Review of Radical Political Economics', IV(3).

REICH, W. (1970), 'The Mass Psychology of Fascism', New York, Farrar, Straus & Giroux.
REISS, A. (1960), The Marginal Status of Adolescents, 'Law and Contemporary Problems', vol.25.
'Report from the Select Committee on Violence in Marriage', vol.1, session 1974-5, London, HMSO.
REYNOLDS, J.M. (1974), Rape as Social Control, 'Catalyst', no.8.
RHINEHART, L. (1972), 'The Dice Man', St Albans, Panther.
RICHARDSON, H. (1969), 'Adolescent Girls in Approved Schools', London, Routledge & Kegan Paul.
ROBINSON, D. (1973), 'Patients, Practitioners and Medical Care', London, Heineman.
ROSE, H. and HANMER, J. (1976), Women's Liberation, Reproduction, and the Technological Fix, in D. Leonard Barker and S. Allen (eds), 'Sexual Divisions and Society: Process and Change', London, Tavistock.
ROTH, B. and LERNER, J. (1975), Sex-Based Discrimination in the Mental Institutionalization of Women, 'California Law Review', vol.62.
ROWBOTHAM, S. (1973), 'Woman's Consciousness, Man's World', Harmondsworth, Penguin.
ROWBOTHAM, S. (1974), 'Hidden from History', London, Pluto Press.
SACHS, A. (forthcoming), 'Sexism and the Law', London, Martin Robertson.
SCHWENDINGER, H. and SCHWENDINGER, J. (1974), Rape Myths: In Legal, Theoretical and Everyday Practice, 'Crime and Social Justice', vol.1.
SCULLY, D. and BART, P. (1973), A Funny Thing Happened on the Way to the Orifice, 'American Journal of Sociology', vol.78, no.4.
SECOMBE, W. (1973), The Housewife and her Labour under Capitalism, 'New Left Review', vol.83.
SHACKLADY, L.A. (1972), 'Female Delinquency and Sex-Role Theory', unpublished MSc thesis, University of Bath.
SHARPE, S. (1976), '"Just Like a Girl": How Girls Learn to be Women', Harmondsworth, Penguin.
SHERFEY, M.J. (1972), 'The Nature and Evolution of Female Sexuality', New York, Random House.
SHORT, J.F. and NYE, F. (1958), The Extent of Unrecorded Juvenile Delinquency, 'Journal of Criminal Law, Criminology and Police Science', vol.49.
SIMON, R.J. (1975), 'Women and Crime', Lexington, D.C. Heath.
SIMON, W. and GAGNON, J.H. (1969), On Psychosexual Development, in D. Goslin (ed.), 'Handbook of Socialization Theory and Research', Chicago, Rand MacNally.
SIMONS, J. (1968), 'African Women, Their Legal Status in Southern Africa', London, Hurst.
SKAPPEL, S. (1922), 'Om Husmandsvaesendet i Norge, dets oprindelse og utvikling' (On the 'Houseman' system in Norway, its origin and development), Videnskapsselskapets skrifter, Kra.
SKULTANS, V. (1975), 'Intimacy and Ritual', London, Routledge & Kegan Paul.
SMART, C. (1976), 'Women, Crime and Criminology: A Feminist Critique', London, Routledge & Kegan Paul.
SMART, C. (1977), Criminological Theory: Its Ideology and Implications concerning Women, 'British Journal of Sociology', vol.28, no.1.

SOOTHILL, K. and JACK, A. (1975), How Rape is Reported, 'New Society', vol.32, no.663.
STEIN, M. (1974), 'Lovers, Friends, Slaves', Berkeley Publishing.
STIMSON, G. (1975), The Message of Psychotropic Drug Ads, 'Journal of Communication', Summer.
STORR, A. (1964), 'Sexual Deviation', Harmondsworth, Penguin.
TAYLOR, G. Rattray, (1965), 'Sex in History', London, Panther.
TERRY, R.M. (1970), Discrimination in the Handling of Juvenile Offenders by Social Control Agencies, in P.G. Garabedian and D.C. Gibbons (eds), 'Becoming Delinquent', New York, Aldine Press.
THOMAS, K. (1959), The Double Standard, 'Journal of the History of Ideas', vol.20, no.2.
THOMAS, W.I. (1907), 'Sex and Society', Boston, Little Brown.
THOMAS, W.I. (1967), 'The Unadjusted Girl', New York, Harper & Row.
THOMASSEN, E. et al. (1976), 'Strukturell veld mot kvinner' (Structural force against women), Stencil 22, Institute of Criminology and Criminal Law, University of Oslo.
TRILLING, L. (1951), 'The Liberal Imagination: Essays on Literature and Society', London, Secker & Warburg.
VEDDER, C.B. and SOMMERVILLE, D.B. (1970), 'The Delinquent Girl', Illinois, Charles C. Thomas.
WADSWORTH, M.E.J. et al. (1971), 'Health and Sickness: the Choice of Treatment', London, Tavistock.
WARD, D., JACKSON, M. and WARD, R. (1969), Crimes of Violence by Women in D. Mulvihill et al. (eds), 'Crimes of Violence', Washington, US Government Printing Office.
WEIS, J.G. (1976), Liberation and Crime: The Invention of the New Female Criminal, 'Crime and Social Justice', vol.6.
WESTLEY, William (1971), 'Violence and the Police: A Sociological Study of Law, Custom and Morality', Boston, MIT Press.
WHYTE, W.F. (1943), A Slum Sex Code, 'American Journal of Sociology' vol.49.
WILSON, E. (1974), 'Women and the Welfare State', Red Rag Pamphlet no.2.
WIMPOLE, Dr R. (1976), Doctor's Diary, 'Woman's Own', 28 August.
WISE, N. (1967), Juvenile Delinquency among Middle-Class Girls, in E. Vaz (ed.), 'Middle Class Juvenile Delinquency', New York, Harper & Row.
WOMEN ENDORSING DECRIMINALIZATION (1973), Prostitution: A Non-Victim Crime?, 'Issues in Criminology', vol.8, no.2.
YERKES, R.M. (1943), 'Chimpanzees', Yale University Press.
YOUNG, W.R., GOY, R. and PHOENIX, C. (1964), Hormones and Sexual Behaviour, 'Science', vol.143, pp.212-18.
ZARETSKY, E. (1976), 'Capitalism, the Family, and Personal Life', London, Pluto Press.
ZIMMER, F. (1975), 'Kvinneskatterett' ('Women and the Tax Law'), Stencil 33, The Institute of Private Law, University of Oslo.
ZOLA, I. (1975), Medicine as an Institution of Social Control, in C. Cox and A. Mead (eds), 'Sociology of Medical Practice', London, Collier Macmillan.

Index

abortion, 15, 24, 41
Amir, M., 92, 100
anti-feminism, 29

broken homes, 75, 80-2
Brownmiller, S., 96-7, 100
Burgess, A.W. and Holstrom, L.L.,
    106

Cambridge Rapist, the, 93, 98,
    99, 103
capitalism, 6, 15, 17, 35, 44
capitalist mode of production, 2,
    3
christianity, 35, 37
Cloward, R.A. and Ohlin, L.E., 66
Cowie, J. et al., 74, 75, 76, 88
criminal process, 2, 72, 80f.,
    108

Davis, Kingsley, 53-4, 55, 62
'The Dice Man', 95
domestic: labour, 3, 6, 14, 32,
    36; sphere, 1, 6, 12f., 34,
    92, 102
double rejection, 84
double standard of morality, 1,
    4-5, 53, 63, 71, 84, 91
Downes, D., 85-6
D.P.P. v Morgan and others, 90
drugs, 20, 21, 43

Ellis, Havelock, 54

family, the, 2, 3, 12, 16, 19-20,
    22, 33, 35, 41, 44, 50, 63

female: criminality, 8f., 21;
    delinquency, 65f., 74f.,
    abnormality of, 74f.,
    sexualization of, 80f.;
    sexuality, 54-5, 56f., 91,
    100, repression of, 61, 64
feminine traits, 62
feudal legacy, 16f.
Flyvel, T.R., 85-6
Freud, S., 62, 64
Friedan, B., 6, 52

Garcia, Inez, 90, 102
general practitioners, 41f.
Goffman, E., 42, 43, 46
Griffin, 89, 100

Henriques, F., 53
Herschberger, R., 57
housewife, 16, 17, 22, 24, 36,
    43, 50-2

imprisonment, 22-3
individual inadequacy, 41, 46,
    75

Jex-Blake, S., 27, 29
Judge Christmas Humphreys, 90,
    100, 102
Judge Edward Sutcliffe, 90,
    100, 102
Judges, 27f., 39; attitude to
    women, 27-8
Judicial: ideology, 13, 32;
    myth, 28, 30; neutrality, 28,
    30

Kinsey, A.C. et al., 54, 55, 57, 58f., 63

law, the, 8, 12, 15, 17, 19, 27f., 39; family, 35; feudal, 36, 38; on prostitution, 62; on rape, 62, 89-90, 91, 109
Law Lords, 90
legal profession, 39
lesbianism, 96
Little, Joan, 90, 102

male: chauvinism, 110; delinquency, 67; dominance, 43, 63; fantasy, 97, 100; ideology, 31, 32; hypocrisy, 33; supremacy, 28
marriage, 14, 16, 17, 35, 54, 70, 71
Married Women's Property Act, 36
masculine traits, 62
Masters, W.M. and Johnson, V.E., 55, 57, 61
Matza, D., 84
medical profession, 3, 4, 29, 30, 39, 41f., 109
menopause, 41
Mill, John Stuart, 28
myth, 31, 37

natural order, 12, 44, 55
news reports, 94
'newsworthiness', 98

Oedipal complex, 64
official criminal statistics, 8, 9, 73, 74, 83
orgasm, 61

patriarchal: family, 63; society, 44, 50
penal system, 2
permissiveness, 53-4, 68
personal troubles, 4, 12, 19, 41, 46, 67
praxis, 107
pregnancy, 3f., 69
pre-marital sex, 68
private prison, the, 21f.
promiscuity, 4-5, 53, 55, 68, 71-4, 84
prostitution, 1, 24, 53f., 62
psychiatrists, 46, 47
'psychosomatic' illness, 41, 45, 46

radical student movement, 104
rape, 1, 8, 19, 25, 62, 63, 64, 89f.; and the cinema, 95-6; and consent, 90; definition of, 91; increase in, 89-90, 104; law on, 62, 89-90, 91, 109; mens rea, 90; planned rape, 92; police attitudes to, 105-6, 108; press reports of, 96f.; trials of, 98; under-reporting of, 89; victim's advocate, 108, 111; victims of, 106, 109, 110, 111; victim precipitation, 93
Rape Crisis Centre, 90, 104-5, 110
Rapists' Charter, 90
repressive triangle, 71, 72
reproduction, 3f., 53, 111
reproduction of labour power, 3, 17
Rhondda, Lady, 27
romantic love, 70, 71

scientific method, 57f.
sex: differences, 76, 84; roles, 10, 13, rejection of, 84
sexual arousal, 58-61, 98-9; 'delinquency', 55, 66, 72, 76, 77-80, 82; perversion, 53, 54; psychopath, 91, 92-3, 99
Sexual Offences (Amendment) Bill, 90
sexuality, 53f., 67, 91, 101
Simon, W. and Gagnon, J.H., 56, 64
sin, 53
Slum Sex Code, 67f.
socialisation, 1, 2, 13, 100
societal reaction, 76, 84-7
socio-economic class, 11, 19-20, 28, 30, 32f., 41, 76, 104-5
Storr, A., 62
subculture, 67, 76, 85f.
suffragettes, 34

tranquillisers, 20, 21, 43

universities, 29, 38

vaginal infections, 51
Victorian men, 28, 34, 63; women, 28, 33, 63

wage labour, 14, 15, 32, 44, 45
welfare provision, 5, 14, 15, 18,
    25, 105
Westley, W., 106
Whyte, W.F., 67f.
wife-battering, 19, 25
women: delicacy of, 31; exclu-
    sion of, 27f.; inequality of,
    1, 39, 91, 99, 110; infer-
    iority of, 29; invisibility
    of, 12, 13, 22; legal status
    of, 5, 18, 38; legislation
    on, 1, 2, 13-14; media images
    of, 94f.; mental constitution
    of, 29; oppression of, 1, 2,
    6, 13; segregation of, 29, 30
women's liberation, 10, 14, 25
Women's Movement, the, 1, 2, 11,
    42, 50, 51, 88
women's self-help health move-
    ment, 42, 43, 51, 104, 105,
    109